BIG DATA

A BUSINESS AND LEGAL GUIDE

BIG DATA

A BUSINESS AND LEGAL GUIDE

JAMES R. KALYVAS
MICHAEL R. OVERLY

CRC Press
Taylor & Francis Group
Boca Raton London New York

CRC Press is an imprint of the
Taylor & Francis Group, an **informa** business

AN AUERBACH BOOK

First published 2015 by CRC Press

Published 2019 by CRC Press
Taylor & Francis Group
6000 Broken Sound Parkway NW, Suite 300
Boca Raton, FL 33487-2742

ISBN-13: 978-1-4665-9237-7 (hbk)

Library of Congress Cataloging-in-Publication Data

Kalyvas, James R. author.
    The law of big data : a legal guide for executives and lawyers / James R. Kalyvas, Michael R. Overly.
      pages cm
    Summary: "Enabling readers to quickly implement solutions with respect to collecting, licensing, handling, and using Big Data, this book provides business people and lawyers with an accessible handbook primer on Big Data and its business implications. All contributors are nationally recognized experts in their fields and each chapter focuses on a different legal issue or risk relating to Big Data. More than a theoretical assessment of issues, the book offers busy people with the means to quickly understand relevant issues and implement specific recommendations to mitigate identified risks. "-- Provided by publisher.
    Includes bibliographical references and index.
    ISBN 978-1-4665-9237-7 (hardback)
    1. Computers--Law and legislation--United States. 2. Data mining--United States. 3. Big data--United States. 4. Business enterprises--Computer networks--United States. 5. Information services--Law and legislation--United States. I. Overly, Michael R. author. II. Title.

KF390.5.C6K35 2014
343.7309'99--dc23
                                                    2014011570

Visit the Taylor & Francis Web site at
http://www.taylorandfrancis.com

and the CRC Press Web site at
http://www.crcpress.com

Dedications

To Julie, Alex, and Zach

For love, joy, and everything important.

—James R. Kalyvas

For my parents.

—Michael R. Overly

Contents

Ethan D. Lenz and Morgan J. Tilleman

Disclaimer

The law changes frequently and rapidly. It is also subject to differing interpretations. It is up to the reader to review the current state of the law with a qualified attorney and other professionals before relying on it. Neither the authors nor the publisher make any guarantees or warranties regarding the outcome of the uses to which the materials in this book are applied. This book is sold with the understanding that the authors and publisher are not engaged in rendering legal or professional services to the reader.

Why We Wrote This Book

"Big Data" is discussed with increasing importance and urgency every day in boardrooms and in other strategic and operational meetings at organizations across the globe. This book starts where the many excellent books and articles on Big Data end—we accept that Big Data will materially change the way businesses and organizations make decisions. Our purpose is to help executives, managers, and counsel to better understand the interrelationships between Big Data and the laws, regulations, and contracting practices that may have an impact on the use of Big Data.

In each chapter of the book, we discuss an area of law that will affect the way your business or organization uses Big Data. We also provide recommendations regarding steps your organization can take to maximize its ability to take advantage of the many opportunities presented by Big Data without creating unforeseen risks and liability to your organization.

This book is not a warning against the use of Big Data. To the contrary, we view Big Data as having the most significant impact on how decisions are made in organizations since the advent of the spreadsheet. Instead, this book is designed to (1) help you think more broadly about the implications of the use of Big Data and (2) assist organizations in establishing procedures to ensure or validate that legal considerations are part of their efforts to harness the power of Big Data.

We have also observed that executives, managers, and counsel may have very different understandings of what Big Data is as compared to the technologists and data scientists in their organizations. The propensity for these different understandings is magnified by the lack of a single accepted definition of Big Data. There is an even less-common understanding among executives, managers, and counsel not involved with technology on a day-to-day basis about how Big Data works. To help address this gap in understanding of Big Data, in Chapter 1 we discuss the definition of Big Data we used in this book, as well as several other popular definitions for comparison. We also provide a Big Data primer, in plain English (from a nontechnical perspective), discussing the characteristics that distinguish Big Data from traditional database models.

Chapters 2 through 11 each take on a specific topic and provide guidance on questions such as

- Can we use Big Data to collect information about our competitors and use it in our pricing decisions without violating antitrust laws?
- Given a single security or privacy breach may subject a business to enforcement actions from a wide range of regulators—not to mention possible claims for damages by customers, business partners, shareholders, and others—how can my organization better understand its information security and privacy compliance obligations?
- How can you mitigate security and privacy risks in your organization?
- How can you include health information as part of your Big Data without violating the patchwork of federal and state laws governing the disclosure and use of health data?
- Can my organization anonymize health information so we can use it with fewer restrictions?
- Can my organization minimize its legal risks by maintaining a clear record of the business purposes of its Big Data analytic efforts?
- How is licensing a database in the context of Big Data different from traditional database licenses, and what are the key licensing considerations?
- Does our insurance provide appropriate coverage for Big Data risks?
- How can we legally leverage Big Data in our hiring decisions?
- Is there a way to meet our discovery hold and electronic discovery obligations in the era of Big Data without breaking the bank?

A final note on how to use this book. The chapters are designed to flow in a logical order, enabling the reader to develop an understanding of how to think about legal issues in connection with Big Data even if a particular law or topic is not specifically addressed. Readers looking for guidance on a particular topic can also refer directly to the relevant chapter. Each chapter stands on its own with regard to its subject matter. Caution should be used in selectively reading chapters as key recommendations and mitigation strategies may be missed.

Acknowledgments

We would like to express our gratitude to our many colleagues who helped with this book. The chapter authors have also recognized colleagues who made significant contributions to individual chapters. In particular, we would like to thank Alexandre C. Nisenbaum and David Albertson for their assistance on multiple chapters; Christine M. Caceres, Shaquille Manley, and Brandon Williams for their assistance with fact gathering; Yvonne Alamillo and Marshann Compfort for their clerical assistance; and Colleen E. Barrett-DeJarnatt and Candice A. Tarantino for their assistance with graphics.

James R. Kalyvas
Michael R. Overly

About the Authors

James R. Kalyvas is a partner with Foley & Lardner LLP and a member of the firm's national Management Committee. He is the firm's chief strategy officer, chair of the firm's Technology Transactions and Outsourcing Practice, and a member of the Technology and Health Care Industry Teams. Mr. Kalyvas advises companies, public entities, and associations on all matters involving the use of information technology, including structuring technology initiatives (e.g., outsourcing, ERP, CRM); vendor selection (RFP strategies, development, and response review); negotiations; technology implementation (professional service agreements, SOWs, and SLAs); and enterprise management of technology assets. Mr. Kalyvas specializes in structuring and negotiating outsourcing transactions, enterprise resource planning initiatives, and unique business partnering relationships. He has incorporated his experience in handling billions of dollars of technology transactions into the development of several proprietary tools relating to the effective management of the technology selection, negotiation, implementation, and management processes. Mr. Kalyvas has been Peer Review Rated as AV® Preeminent™, the highest performance rating in Martindale–Hubbell's peer review rating system and in 2010–2013, the *Legal 500* recognized him for his technology work, specifically in the areas of outsourcing and transactions. In addition, Mr. Kalyvas was recognized in *Chambers USA* for his technology transactions and outsourcing work (2012 and 2013), and the International Association of Outsourcing Professionals recognized Foley & Lardner on its 2013 "World's Best Outsourcing Advisor" list. Mr. Kalyvas has authored articles and books relating to software licensing and the negotiation of information systems. He coauthored the publication *Software Agreements Line by Line* (Aspatore Books, 2004) and *Negotiating Telecommunications Agreements Line by Line* (Aspatore Books, 2005). Together with colleagues in his practice, Mr. Kalyvas coauthored the whitepaper "Cloud Computing: A Practical Framework for Managing Cloud Computing Risk."

Michael R. Overly is a partner in the Technology Transactions and Outsourcing Practice Group in Foley & Lardner's Los Angeles office. As an attorney and former electrical engineer, his practice focuses on counseling clients regarding technology licensing, intellectual property development, information security, and electronic commerce. Mr. Overly is one of the few practicing lawyers who has satisfied the rigorous requirements necessary to obtain the Certified Information Systems Auditor (CISA), Certified Information Systems Security Professional (CISSP), Information Systems Security Management Professional (ISSMP), Certified in Risk and Information Systems Controls (CRISC), and Certified Information Privacy Professional (CIPP) certifications. He is a member of the Computer Security Institute and the Information Systems Security Association. Mr. Overly is a frequent writer and speaker in many areas, including negotiating and drafting technology transactions and the legal issues of technology in the workplace, email, and electronic evidence. He has written numerous articles and books on these subjects and is a frequent commentator in the national press (e.g., *The New York Times, Chicago Tribune, Los Angeles Times, Wall Street Journal,* ABCNEWS.com, CNN, and MSNBC). In addition to conducting training seminars in the United States, Norway, Japan, and Malaysia, Mr. Overly has testified before the US Congress regarding online issues. Among others, he is the author of the best-selling *e-policy: How to Develop Computer, Email, and Internet Guidelines to Protect Your Company and Its Assets* (AMACOM, 1998), *Overly on Electronic Evidence* (West Publishing, 2002), *The Open Source Handbook* (Pike & Fischer, 2003), *Document Retention in the Electronic Workplace* (Pike & Fischer, 2001), and *Licensing Line by Line* (Aspatore Press, 2004).

Contributors

David R. Albertson is an associate with Foley & Lardner LLP and a member of the firm's Technology Transactions and Outsourcing and Privacy, Security, and Information Management Practices. His practice focuses on counseling clients regarding technology transactions, intellectual property protection, and data privacy and information security compliance issues. He is a Certified Information Privacy Professional in Information Technology (CIPP/IT), certified by the International Association of Privacy Professionals.

Benjamin R. Dryden is an associate in the Washington, D.C., office of Foley & Lardner LLP and a member of the firm's Antitrust and eDiscovery and Data Management Practice Groups. He represents clients in antitrust merger reviews and complex litigation.

Howard W. Fogt is a partner in the Washington, D.C., and Brussels, Belgium, offices of Foley & Lardner LLP and is a member of the firm's Antitrust and International Practice Groups. He counsels and represents corporate clients in antitrust aspects of multinational mergers and acquisitions and international and domestic antitrust compliance and conduct matters.

M. Leeann Habte is an associate with Foley & Lardner LLP, where she is a member of the Health Care Industry Team. She is also a Certified Information Privacy Professional (CIPP) and a member of the firm's Privacy, Security, and Information Management Practice. A former director at the University of California at Los Angeles and the Minnesota Department of Health, she has practical experience in developing and implementing data privacy and security policies and procedures and managing information technology resources.

Chanley T. Howell is a partner with Foley & Lardner LLP, where he practices privacy, security, and information technology law. He is a Certified Information Privacy Professional (CIPP) and regularly represents clients in connection with privacy and security compliance and complex information technology transactions.

Ethan D. Lenz is a member of Foley & Lardner's Insurance Industry Team, as well as the Insurance and Reinsurance Litigation Practice. His practice focuses on providing risk management and insurance coverage–related advice to many of the firm's commercial clients, including advice relative to the negotiation and structure of a wide variety of commercial/professional insurance programs. He is a regular speaker on insurance-related topics, including current issues affecting directors and officers liability insurance, captive insurance companies, and other commercial insurance products.

Adam C. Losey is an attorney, author, and educator in the field of technology law. He is the president and editor-in-chief of IT-Lex (http://it-lex.org), a technology law 501(c)(3) not-for-profit educational and literary organization, and for several years, he served as an adjunct professor at Columbia University, where he taught electronic discovery as part of Columbia's information and digital resource management master's program.

Mark J. Neuberger is Of Counsel in the Miami office of Foley & Lardner LLP, where he represents management in all aspects of labor and employment law. His practical insights into employment law were gained in part from his prior ten years' experience in progressively responsible human resource management positions for what was then a Fortune 100 company. He has a bachelor of science degree in industrial and labor relations from Cornell University and a juris doctor from Duquesne University.

Eileen R. Ridley is a partner in Foley & Lardner LLP's San Francisco office. She is a member of the firm's national Management Committee, the cochair of the firm's Privacy, Security, and Information Management practice and a vice chair of the Litigation Department. Ridley is a trial lawyer dealing with complex commercial disputes, including class actions and multidistrict litigation. Ridley has handled a wide variety of privacy disputes, including internal investigations, breach responses, and consumer and competitor litigation.

Alan D. Rutenberg is a partner in the Washington, D.C., office of Foley & Lardner LLP and chairs the firm's Antitrust Practice Group. He focuses his practice on antitrust issues arising from mergers and acquisitions and conduct matters, antitrust litigation, and antitrust counseling. He regularly represents clients in antitrust matters before the Federal Trade Commission and the Department of Justice.

Aaron K. Tantleff is a partner in Foley & Lardner LLP's Technology Transactions and Outsourcing practice group and a member of the firm's Privacy, Security, and Information Management and Health Care, Life Sciences, and Energy Industry Teams. He has represented companies in technology and outsourcing transactions, both as in-house and outside counsel. Prior to joining Foley, he served as in-house counsel for a global software company and for a global information technology and management consulting company. He is a frequent speaker in the area of technology and outsourcing transactions, including recent developments and best practices for drafting and negotiating contracts.

Morgan J. Tilleman is an associate at Foley & Lardner LLP and a member of the firm's Insurance Industry Team. His practice focuses on providing corporate and regulatory counsel to the insurance industry, including mergers and acquisitions, reinsurance, licensing, premium taxation, and compliance issues.

1

A Big Data Primer for Executives

James R. Kalyvas

1.1 WHAT IS BIG DATA?

The phrase *Big Data* is commonplace in business discussions, yet it does not have a universally understood meaning. The main objective of this chapter is to provide a simple framework for understanding Big Data.

There have been many different definitions for Big Data proposed by technology experts and a wide range of organizations. For purposes of this book, we developed the following definition:

> Big Data is a process to deliver decision-making insights. The process uses people and technology to quickly analyze large amounts of data of different types (traditional table structured data and unstructured data, such as pictures, video, email, transaction data, and social media interactions) from a variety of sources to produce a stream of actionable knowledge.

Because there is no commonly accepted definition of Big Data, we offer this definition because it is both descriptive and practical. Our definition emphasizes that the term *Big Data* really refers to a process that results in information that supports decision making, and the definition underscores that Big Data is not simply a shorthand reference to an amount or type of data. Our definition is derived from our research and elements of a number of existing definitions.

We include several frequently referenced definitions next for context and comparison. According to the McKinsey Global Institute:

> "Big Data" refers to datasets whose size is beyond the ability of typical database software tools to capture, store, manage, and analyze. This definition is intentionally subjective and incorporates a moving definition of how

big a dataset needs to be in order to be considered Big Data—i.e., we don't define Big Data in terms of being larger than a certain number of terabytes (thousands of gigabytes). We assume that, as technology advances over time, the size of datasets that qualify as Big Data will also increase. Also note that the definition can vary by sector, depending on what kinds of software tools are commonly available and what sizes of datasets are common in a particular industry. With those caveats, Big Data in many sectors today will range from a few dozen terabytes to multiple petabytes (thousands of terabytes). (McKinsey Global Institute. *Big Data: The Next Frontier for Innovation, Competition, and Productivity.* McKinsey & Company, June 2011.)

Gartner indicates the following:

Big Data is high-volume, high-velocity and high-variety information assets that demand cost-effective, innovative forms of information processing for enhanced insight and decision making. (Gartner. IT Glossary. 2013. http://www.gartner.com/it-glossary/big-data/.)

The term *Big Data* is sometimes used in this book as part of a phrase, such as "Big Data analytics," when a particular part of the process is being emphasized. In the rest of this chapter, we continue to build on the framework for understanding Big Data and describe at a very high level and in relatively nontechnical terms how it works.

1.1.1 Characteristics of Big Data

You will rarely see a discussion of Big Data that does not include a reference to the "3 Vs"[1]—volume, velocity, and variety—as distinguishing characteristics of Big Data. Simply put, it is the volume (amount of data), velocity (the speed of processing and the pace of change to data), and variety (sources of data and types of data)[2] that most notably distinguish Big Data from the traditional approaches used to capture, store, manage, and analyze data.

1.1.2 Volume

The volume of data available to enterprises has dramatically increased since 2004. In 2004, the total amount of data stored on the entire Internet was 1 petabyte (equivalent to 100 years of all television content). As can be seen in Figure 1.1, by 2011 the total worldwide amount of information

Visualizing Big Data

1 bit
Single choice or decision:
yes/no, black/white

1 byte
(8 bits)
Single character on a
computer keyboard

1 kilobyte
(1,024 bytes)
Two to three
paragraphs of text

1 megabyte
(1,048,576 bytes)
Text of a brief
novel

1 gigabyte
(1,073,741,824 bytes)
Twelve banker's boxes of
text-based documents

1 terabyte
(1,000 gigabytes)
Text on 250 million double-sided
pages — a stack that would reach
over 10 miles high

1 petabyte
(1,000 terabytes)
100 years of all
television content

1 exabyte
(1,000 petabytes)
Data on a stack
of CD ROMs
1,864 miles high

1 zettabyte
(1,000 exabytes)
Total amount of information stored electronically as of
2011 or 36 million years of HD video

1 yottabyte = **33x**
(1,000 zettabytes)

predicted total volume of all
global data that will exist in the
year 2019

FIGURE 1.1
Visualizing Big Data.

stored electronically was 1 zettabyte (1 million petabytes or 36 million years of high-definition [HD] video). By 2015, that number is estimated to reach 7.9 zettabytes (or 7.9 million petabytes), and then by 2003 sky-rocket to 35 zettabytes (or 35 million petabytes).[3] The size of the datasets in use today, and continually and exponentially growing, has outpaced the capabilities of traditional data tools to capture, store, manage, and analyze the data.

1.1.3 The Internet of Things and Volume

The volume of data to be stored and analyzed will experience another dramatic upward arc as more and more objects are equipped with sensors that generate and relay data without the need for human inter-action. Known as the Internet of Things (IoT), a concept hailing from the Massachusetts Institute of Technology (MIT) since 2000, it is the ability for machines and other objects, through sensors or other implanted devices, to communicate relevant data through the Internet directly to connected machines. The IoT is already in action regularly today (think exercise devices such as Fitbit® or FuelBand or connected appliances like the Nest thermostat or smoke detector), and we are still at the early stages of how ubiquitous it will become. For example, a basketball was recently produced with sensors that provide direct feedback to the user on the arc, spin, and speed of release of the player's shots. While the player is receiving instant feedback and even "coaching" from the app on his or her iPhone, the app is also sending all of this data to the manufacturer as well as other important data relating to the frequency and duration of use, places the user frequents to play; by matching weather information, the manufacturer can even collect information on the impact of weather con-ditions on the performance characteristics of the ball. Regardless of how, or whether, the manufacturer uses these insights, it has unprecedented ability to interact with and obtain multiple types of feedback directly from the basketball, and all the player does is connect it and use it.

1.1.4 Variety

Big Data is also transforming data analytics by dramatically expanding the variety of useful data to analyze. Big Data combines the value of data stored in traditional structured[4] databases with the value of the wealth of new data available from sources of unstructured data. Unstructured data includes the rapidly growing universe of data that is not structured. Common examples of unstructured data are user-generated content from social media (e.g., Facebook, Twitter, Instagram, and Tumblr), images, videos, surveillance data, sensor data, call center information, geo-location data, weather data, economic data, government data and reports, research, Internet search trends, and web log files. Today, more than 95% of all data that exists globally is estimated to be unstructured data. These data sources can provide extremely valuable business intelligence. Using Big Data analytics, organizations can now make correlations and uncover patterns in the data that could not have been identified through conventional methods.[5] The correlations and patterns can provide a company with insight on external conditions that have a direct impact on an enterprise, such as market trends, consumer behaviors, and operational efficiencies, as well as identify interdependencies between the conditions.

1.1.5 Velocity

A rapidly ever-increasing amount of unstructured data from an exponentially growing number of sources streams continuously across the Internet. The speed with which this data must be stored and analyzed constitutes the velocity characteristic of Big Data.

1.1.6 Validation

If you are counting, you will note that "validation" is a fourth *V*. We have added this fourth *V* for your consideration because it captures one of the core teachings of this book: An organization's Big Data strategy must include a validation step. This validation step should be used by the organization to insert appropriate pauses in their analytics efforts to assess how laws, regulations, or contractual obligations have an impact on the

- Architecture of Big Data systems
- Design of Big Data search algorithms
- Actions to be taken based on the derived insights
- Storage and distribution of the results and data

Each of the chapters addresses applicable legal considerations to illustrate the importance of validation and provides recommendations for effective validation steps.

1.2. CROSS-DISCIPLINARY APPROACH, NEW SKILLS, AND INVESTMENT

Organizations that seek to leverage Big Data in their operations will also need to develop cross-disciplinary teams that wed deep knowledge of the business with technology. An essential component of these teams will be the data scientist. Whether the data scientist is an employee or a contractor, he or she is essential to extracting the promise of business insights Big Data holds for organizations (i.e., deriving order and knowledge from the chaos that can be Big Data). The data scientist is a multidimensional thinker who operates effectively in talking about business issues in business terms while also at the apex of technology and statistics education and experience. The role of the data scientist is captured well in the following excerpts from a job posting for the position from a leading consumer manufacturing company:[6]

Key Responsibilities:

- Analyze large datasets to develop custom models and algorithms to drive business solutions
- Build complex datasets from multiple data sources
- Build learning systems to analyze and filter continuous data flows and offline data analysis
- Develop custom data models to drive innovative business solutions
- Conduct advanced statistical analysis to determine trends and significant data relationships
- Research new techniques and best practices within the industry

Technology Skills:

- Having the ability to query databases and perform statistical analysis
- Being able to develop or program databases
- Being able to create examples, prototypes, demonstrations to help management better understand the work
- Having a good understanding of design and architecture principles
- Strong experience in data warehousing and reporting
- Experience with multiple RDBMS (Relational Database Management Systems) and physical database schema design
- Experience in relational and dimensional modeling
- Process and technology fluency with key analytic applications (for example, customer relationship management, supply chain management and financials)

- Familiar with development tools (e.g., MapReduce, Hadoop, Hive) and programming languages (e.g., C++, Java, Python, Perl)
- Very data driven and ability to slice and dice large volumes of data

The data scientist is not the only subject matter expert needed in designing a Big Data strategy but plays a critical role. The data scientist will work with business subject matter experts from your organization as well as the data architects and analysts, technology infrastructure team, management, and others to deliver Big Data insights. Whether your organization elects to build or buy Big Data capabilities, there is a strategic investment that must be made to acquire new analytical skill sets and develop cross-functional teams to execute on your Big Data objectives.

1.3 ACQUIRING RELEVANT DATA

Organizations will need to gain access to data that will be relevant to the objectives they are trying to achieve with Big Data. This data can be available from any number of sources, including from existing databases throughout an organization or enterprise, from local or remote storage systems, directly from public sources on the Internet or from the government or trade associations, by license from a third party, or from third-party data brokers or providers that remotely aggregate and host valuable sources of data. Ultimately, organizations will need to ensure that they can legally obtain and maintain access to these data sources over time so that they will be able to continually reassess their results and make meaningful comparisons and not lose access to valuable business intelligence.

1.4 THE BASICS OF HOW BIG DATA TECHNOLOGY WORKS

A growing number of proprietary and open-solution (i.e., publicly available without charge) Big Data analytic platforms are available to enterprises, as well as hosted solutions. For the sole purpose of simplicity in trying to describe how the technology behind Big Data works, we focus on

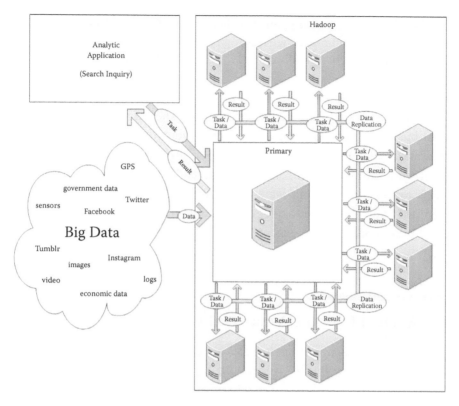

FIGURE 1.2
Simplified Hadoop distributed computing cluster illustration

Apache's™ Hadoop® software in this discussion. Hadoop is an open-source application generally made available without license fees to the public.

Hadoop (reportedly named after the favorite stuffed animal of the child of one of its creators) is a popular open-source framework consisting of a number of software tools used to perform Big Data analytics. Hadoop takes the very large data distribution and analytic tasks inherent in Big Data and breaks them down into smaller and more manageable pieces. Hadoop accomplishes this by enabling an organization to connect many smaller and lower-price computers together to work in parallel as a single cost-effective computing cluster. Hadoop automatically distributes data across all of the computers on the cluster as the data is being loaded, so there is no need to first aggregate the data separately on a storage-area network (SAN) or otherwise (Figure 1.2). At the same time the data is being distributed, each block of data is replicated on several of the computers in the cluster. So, as Hadoop is breaking down the computing task into many pieces, it is also minimizing the chances that data will not be available when needed by making the data available on multiple computers. Each of these features offers efficiencies over traditional computer architectures.[7] Of course, setting up this distributed computing structure with Hadoop, or similar tools, requires an initial investment that may not be warranted if your computer cluster is smaller. However, once the initial investment in a platform like Hadoop is made, it can be incrementally expanded to include more computers (scaled) at a low cost per increment.

Hadoop is a combination of advanced software and computer hardware, often referred to as a "platform," that provides organizations with a means of executing a "client application." These applications are the actual source of the code or scripts that are written to specifically describe the analytic functions (tasks) that Hadoop will be performing and the data on which those tasks will be performed.[8] The analytic applications that use platforms like Hadoop to analyze Big Data are not typically focused on analysis that requires explicit direct relationships between already well-defined data structures, such as would be required by an accounting system, for example. Instead, by performing statistical analysis and modeling on the data, these applications are focused on uncovering patterns, unknown correlations, and other useful information in the data that may never have been identified using traditional relational data models.

When a computer on the cluster completes its assigned processing task, it returns its results and any related data back to the central computer and then requests another task. The individual results and data are reassembled by the central computer so that they can be returned to the client application or stored elsewhere on Hadoop's file system or database.

1.5 SUMMARY

To develop an explanation of Big Data suitable for its purpose in this book, we greatly simplified the discussion of how the complex technologies behind Big Data work. But, the purpose of this chapter was not to act as a blueprint for constructing a Big Data platform in your organization. Instead, we provided a basic and common understanding of what the phrase *Big Data* really means so that the frequent uses of the term throughout the remaining chapters can be read in that context.

NOTES

1. Although ubiquitous now, the origin of the 3V's is regularly attributed to Gartner Incorporated.
2. Douglas Laney. 3D Data Management: Controlling Data Volume, Velocity and Variety. Gartner, February 6, 2001. Blogs.gartner.com/doug-laney/files/2012/01/ad949-3D-Data-Management-Controlling-Data-Volume-Velocity-and-Variety.pdf
3. Eaton et al. Understanding Big Data: Analytics for Enterprise Class Hadoop and Streaming Data (IBM). New York: McGraw, 2012.
4. Michael Cooper and Peter Mell. Tackling Big Data. NIST Information Technology Laboratory Computer Security Division. http://csrc.nist.gov/groups/SMA/forum/documents/june2012presentations/fcsm_june2012_cooper_mell.pdf.
5. Michael Cooper and Peter Mell. Tackling Big Data. NIST Information Technology Laboratory Computer Security Division. http://csrc.nist.gov/groups/SMA/forum/documents/june2012presentations/fcsm_june2012_cooper_mell.pdf.
6. IT Data Scientist Job Description (The Clorox Company), http: //www.linkedin.com/jobs2/view/9495684
7. First, the cost of improving the density of processors and hard disks on a large enterprise server becomes disproportionately more expensive than building an equally capable cluster of smaller computers. Second, the rate at which modern hard drives can read and write data has not advanced as fast as has the storage capacity of hard disks or the speed of processors. Finally, in contrast to the distributed approach used in Big Data, enterprise relational database systems must first sequence and organize data before it can be loaded, and these systems are commonly subject to time-consuming processes like lengthy extract-transform-load (ETL) processes that could hinder system performance or delay data collection by hours or may even require importing old data with incremental batching and other manual processes.
8. Although the analogy of a search query is useful, a user of a search engine is actually receiving the final product of a complex Big Data analytic process by which the search engine scoured the Internet for data, indexed that data, and stored it for rapid retrieval. If you would like to learn more about the application of advanced analytics, we recommend reviewing *Analytics at Work: Smarter Decisions, Better Results* by Thomas H. Davenport and Jeanne G. Harris.

2

Overview of Information Security and Compliance: Seeing the Forest for the Trees

Michael R. Overly

2.1 INTRODUCTION

Businesses today are faced with the almost-insurmountable task of complying with a confusing array of laws and regulations relating to data privacy and security. These can come from a variety of sources: local, state, national, and even international lawmakers. Information security standards not only are established through laws and regulations but also may be created by contractual standards such as the Payment Card Industry Data Security Standard (PCI DSS) and even common industry standards for information security published by organizations like the Computer Emergency Response Team (CERT) at Carnegie Mellon, and the families of standards from the International Organization for Standardization (ISO).

In many instances, laws and regulations are vague and ambiguous, with little specific guidance regarding compliance. Worse yet, the laws of different jurisdictions may be, and frequently are, conflicting. One state or country may require security measures that are entirely different from those of another state or country. Reconciling all of these legal obligations can be, at best, a full-time job and, at worst, the subject of fines, penalties, and lawsuits.

In response to the growing threat to data security, regulators in literally every jurisdiction have enacted or are in the process of enacting laws and regulations to impose data security and privacy obligations on businesses. Even within a single jurisdiction, a number of government entities may all have authority to take action against a business that fails to comply with applicable standards. That is, a single security breach might subject a business to enforcement actions from a wide range of regulators, not to mention possible claims for damages by customers, business partners, shareholders, and others. The United States, for example, uses a sector-based approach to protect the privacy and security of personal information (e.g., separate federal laws exist relating to health care, financial, credit worthiness, student, and children's personal information). Other approaches, for example in the European Union, provide a unified standard but offer heightened protection for certain types of highly sensitive information (e.g., health care information, sexual orientation, union membership). Actual implementation of the standards into law is dependent on the member country. Canada uses a similar approach in its Personal Information Protection and Electronic Documents Act ("PIPEDA"). Liability for fines and damages can easily run into millions of dollars. Even if liability is relatively limited, the company's business reputation may be irreparably harmed from the adverse publicity and loss in customer and business partner confidence.

The challenges of compliance with this ever-increasing morass of laws, regulations, standards, and contractual obligations can be overwhelming, particularly in the context of Big Data, for which the volume and variety of data might implicate dozens of potentially conflicting obligations and standards. Even if no personally identifiable information is at risk, businesses have obligations to protect other highly sensitive information relating to, for example, their trade secrets, marketing efforts, business partner interactions, and so on.

Although there are no easy solutions, this chapter seeks to achieve several goals:

- To make clear that privacy relating to personal information is only one element of compliance. Businesses also have obligations to protect a variety of other types of data (e.g., trade secrets, data and information of business partners, nonpublic financial information, etc.).
- To sift through various privacy and security laws, regulations, and standards to identify three common, relatively straightforward threads that run through many of them:

    1. The confidentiality, integrity, and availability (CIA) requirement that has been a fundamental precept of information security for many, many years;

2. Acting "reasonably" or taking "appropriate" or "necessary" measures to protect sensitive information; and
3. Scaling security measures to reflect the sensitivity of the information and magnitude of the threat presented (e.g., "one size fits all" is not an appropriate approach to information security and privacy).

By understanding these high-level concepts, businesses can better understand their overall information security and compliance obligations.

2.2 WHAT KIND OF DATA SHOULD BE PROTECTED?

In thinking about information security, the natural first thought is of personally identifiable data or personal information. Although it is certainly true that most laws and regulations focus on personal information, this is only one type of data for which businesses may have legal obligations. Almost every business will have a wide variety of highly sensitive information that must be secured. Some examples include the following:

- **General confidential information of the business.** This could include financial information, marketing plans, potential promotional activities, business contact information, investor information, new product plans, customer lists, and so on.
- **Intellectual property** frequently makes up one of the most, if not *the* most, substantial asset of businesses. A breach of security could result in the business forever losing its ability to enforce its intellectual property rights. For example, trade secrets are defined as sensitive information of a business that has value because it is not generally known in the industry and is the subject of efforts by the business to ensure it remains confidential (e.g., the formula for Coca-Cola®). If a trade secret is revealed to the public, it loses its status and value as a trade secret. Almost every business has at least some trade secrets. A customer list, software source code, formulas, methods of doing business, and so on can all be trade secrets. These must be secured to ensure the information remains protected as a trade secret.
- **Health care information** is one of the most highly regulated and sensitive types of information. In the United States, for example, the Health Insurance Portability and Accountability Act (HIPAA)

regulates the privacy and security of personal health information. In some jurisdictions, it is afforded the highest protection in comparison with other types of personal data. In the European Union, health care information is afforded heightened protection under the European Union Data Protection Directive, as reflected in the member countries' implementing laws. See also the Australian Privacy Act 1988 and recent Privacy Amendment (Enhancing Privacy Protection) Act. A business may be in the health care industry and have possession of actual patient records, but even a business that has nothing to do with the health care industry may have health care information of its employees (e.g., insurance claim information) that it is obligated to protect.

- Like health care information, **personal financial information** is also heavily regulated and highly sensitive. In the United States, the Gramm-Leach-Bliley Act (GLBA) addresses the privacy and security of personal financial information. In other countries, personal information is broadly defined in overarching laws to encompass almost anything identifiable to an individual, including, of course, financial information. See, for example, Japan's Personal Information Protection Act. As with health care information, a business need not be in the financial services industry to possess this type of information. Every employer has sensitive financial information of its employees (e.g., salary information, Social Security and other personal identification numbers, bank account numbers, etc.).

- Even **security information**, itself, is sensitive and should be protected. The security policies, security audit reports, disaster recovery and business continuity plans, and other similar information of a business are all highly sensitive. If compromised, the information could be used to exploit vulnerabilities in the business.

2.3 WHY PROTECTIONS ARE IMPORTANT

Legal compliance is certainly at the very top of every business' list in terms of reasons to implement information security measures to protect sensitive data. However, there are other, significant, reasons for businesses to address this risk:

- **Protecting Corporate Assets**. As noted in the preceding section, in addition to personally identifiable data, every business also has other, highly proprietary information that it must protect (e.g., intellectual property, marketing plans, new product plans, investor information, financial information, etc.). These are all valuable assets of the business, deserving of protection.

- **Establishing Diligence**. Many laws and regulations include the concept of requiring the business to act with due diligence in protecting sensitive data. The same concept exists more generally in the obligation of corporate management to act with due care and to exercise reasonable judgment in conducting the business, which would include acting with due diligence in protecting corporate information assets. Neither applicable law nor this more general corporate governance standard requires perfection. Rather, the business and its managers must be able to demonstrate they acted reasonably, appropriately, and with due diligence in protecting their information assets. By implementing and documenting a thoughtful approach to mitigating information security risks, the business and its managers will have evidence to support they did just that in the event of a breach.

- **Protecting Business Reputation**. Being the subject of a security breach can dramatically harm the reputation of a business. Adverse publicity of this kind could seriously harm a business. Customers and business partners may lose confidence in the ability of the business to protect their information and secure their systems.

- **Minimize Potential Liability**. Finally, the most obvious reason for implementing a thoughtful approach to information security is minimizing potential liability. Liability can take many forms: fines by a variety of regulators, statutory sanctions, shareholder lawsuits, and civil suits by business partners and customers (including the possibility of costly class action lawsuits) against both the business and, potentially, its management.

2.4 COMMON MISCONCEPTIONS ABOUT INFORMATION SECURITY COMPLIANCE

There is much confusion and many misconceptions when it comes to information security compliance. The two biggest misconceptions are that "it's *all* about the data" and "it's *all* about confidentiality." While data and confidentiality are certainly of critical importance, a more holistic approach is required. A business must be concerned about its data, but it must be equally concerned about the systems on which the data resides. In addition, confidentiality is only one of the three key protections required for true security.

Anyone involved in information security should be familiar with the acronym CIA, which stands for confidentiality, integrity, and availability. For data to be truly secure, each of these three elements must be satisfied.

- **Confidentiality** means the data is protected from unauthorized access and disclosure. This is the most obvious of the three requirements in CIA.
- **Integrity** means the data can be relied on as accurate and that it has not been subject to unauthorized alteration. Consider the importance of the integrity element in the context of Big Data: If the data cannot be relied on because certain elements may have been altered, the entire database is rendered suspect.
- Finally, **availability** means the data is available for access and use when required. It does no good to have data that is confidential and the integrity maintained, but the data is not actually available when a user requires it. To achieve this last requirement, the systems on which the data resides must have specific service levels for availability, response time, and so on. This is particularly important when a third-party vendor may be hosting the data for the benefit of the business.

The importance of CIA cannot be overstated. It is not just a concept in information security treatises. Lawmakers have directly incorporated that very language into certain information security laws and regulations. Businesses that fail to achieve CIA with regard to their data may be found in violation of those laws.

A final misconception about information security and privacy laws is that they require perfection (i.e., any breach, regardless of how diligent the business has been, will create liability). This is not true. The laws and regulations in this area are directed at having businesses do what is reasonable and appropriate. If the business achieves that standard and a breach nonetheless occurs, it will generally not have a compliance problem.

2.5 FINDING COMMON THREADS
IN COMPLIANCE LAWS AND REGULATIONS

The sheer number and variety of laws, regulations, and other standards governing the handling of sensitive information can be daunting, if not overwhelming. In some instances, it may be almost impossible for even a large, sophisticated organization to identify all applicable requirements, reconcile inconsistencies, and then implement a compliance program. In this section, the goal is not to discuss any specific laws or regulations but to identify three common threads that run through many of them. By understanding those common threads, businesses can more easily understand their baseline compliance obligations.[1]

As mentioned in the introduction to the chapter, there are three common threads to consider. These threads run through not only laws and regulations but also contractual standards such as the PCI DSS and, even, common industry standards for information security published by organizations like CERT at Carnegie Mellon and the families of standards furnished by ISO. Embracing these common threads in designing and implementing an overall approach to information will greatly increase the ability of a business to achieve overall compliance with the laws, regulations, and other requirements applicable to it.

- **CIA.** As discussed, the well-established, foundational concept of CIA found in every handbook on information security has now been codified into many laws and regulations. The three prongs of this concept address the most fundamental goals of information security: The data/information must be maintained in confidence, it must be protected against unauthorized modification, and it must be available for use when needed. The lack of any of the foregoing protections would materially have an impact on compliance and the value of the information asset.
- **Acting "reasonably" or taking "appropriate" or "necessary" measures.** The concept of acting reasonably is used in many state and federal laws in the United States, Australia, and many other countries. The related concept of acting to take appropriate or necessary measures is used in the European Union and many other areas. Together, they form the heart of almost every information security and data privacy law. A business must act reasonably or do what is necessary or

appropriate to protect its data. Note that this does *not* require perfection. Rather, as discussed in the next paragraph, the business must take into account the risk presented and do what is reasonable or necessary to mitigate that risk. If a breach nonetheless occurs, provided the business has established this basic requirement, it will not be generally found in violation of the applicable law or regulation.

- **Scaling security measures to reflect the nature of the data and threat.** A concept that is closely related to acting reasonably or doing what is appropriate is the idea of scaling security measures to reflect the nature of the threat and sensitivity of the data. That is, a business need not spend the entirety of its security budget to address a low-risk threat. But, if the risk is substantial, particularly in light of the volume or sensitivity of the data, the level of effort and expenditure by the business to address that risk must increase. A database with only names and physical addresses may not require as much security as a database of names, addresses, and Social Security numbers. To better understand this concept, here are excerpts from two laws that incorporate "scaling." The first is from the Massachusetts Data Security Law:

Safeguards that are appropriate to (a) the size, scope and type of business of the person obligated to safeguard the personal information under such comprehensive information security program; (b) the amount of resources available to such person; (c) the amount of stored data; and (d) the need for security and confidentiality of both consumer and employee information.

The second example is from the HIPAA Security Rule and gives the following factors to consider:

(i) The size, complexity, and capabilities of the Covered Entity.
(ii) The Covered Entity's technical infrastructure, hardware, and software security capabilities.
(iii) The costs of security measures.
(iv) The probability and criticality of potential risks to ePHI (ePHI refers to protected health information in electronic form).

2.6 CONCLUSION

Although the number and complexity of privacy and information security laws, regulations, and other standards is ever increasing, businesses should appreciate certain common threads that run through them. In this chapter, three of the most common and most important threads were presented. By understanding that current law does not require perfection but only due care, reasonableness, and scaling measures to reflect the sensitivity of the data being placed at risk, businesses can go a long way to achieving compliance.

NOTE

1. Of course, businesses must ensure overall compliance with the laws and regulations applicable to them. The goal here is to identify the common ground found in many of those laws and regulations to afford businesses with a high-level view of compliance obligations.

3

Information Security in Vendor and Business Partner Relationships

Michael R. Overly

Michael R. Overly

3.1 INTRODUCTION

Entrusting any amount of sensitive information to a business partner or vendor should always involve not only an assessment of applicable privacy issues (discussed in Chapter 4) but also overall information security measures to secure the information. In the context of Big Data, the size and sensitivity of the databases make this issue all the more important. Worse yet, these databases create an almost irresistible target for hackers and others with malicious intent.

The issue of information security should be at the forefront in any instance when Big Data may be licensed or otherwise made accessible to a third party. As noted, those third parties may be business partners to whom a database is licensed, a hosting provider who will have physical possession of the database, a hardware vendor who will service the servers on which the database resides, or any other vendor or service provider who will have contact with or possession of the database or the equipment on which it is stored.

All too frequently, however, the agreements with these third parties are entered into without having performed substantial due diligence and without adequately addressing information security in the relevant contracts, in many instances leaving the business without a meaningful remedy for the substantial harm it may suffer in the event a compromise of security results in unauthorized use or disclosure of the database. Newspapers and trade journals feature a growing number of stories detailing instances in which organizations have entrusted their databases to a third party only to see that information compromised because the third party failed to implement appropriate information security safeguards. The resulting harm can be dramatic: loss of trade secret status, damage to business reputation, loss of business, lost profits, regulatory sanctions, and so on.

3.2 CHAPTER OVERVIEW

This chapter discusses three tools, developed through the negotiation of hundreds of transactions involving the use and possession of databases, that database owners can use to mitigate the risk of entrusting third parties with access to their information. Those tools are the following:

- **Due Diligence Questionnaire**. A due diligence questionnaire designed to document and identify third-party practices with regard to information security and other related matters;
- **Contractual Protections**. Key contractual protections that go beyond a basic license grant and confidentiality clause; and
- **Information Security Requirements**. In appropriate circumstances, the inclusion of an exhibit detailing information security requirements for the engagement.

Whenever a third party will have access to the network, facilities, or databases of a business, one or more of these tools should be considered as part of the contracting process with that third party.

Use of these tools will enable a business to achieve a number of important goals:

- Reduce the risk of security breaches with regard to its data.
- Protect the value of its databases.
- Create contractual remedies in the event of a security breach.
- Establish that the business has used due care and has been diligent in protecting its data. In the event of a compromise, the tools described in this chapter will assist the business in documenting its efforts to minimize risk.
- Protect the reputation of the business and avoid the public embarrassment associated with a security compromise.

3.3 THE FIRST TOOL: A DUE DILIGENCE QUESTIONNAIRE

Businesses may potentially conduct some form of due diligence before entrusting third parties with their data; however, the due diligence process is often done informally and in a nonuniform manner and is seldom properly documented. In very few instances is the outcome of that due diligence actually incorporated into the parties' ultimate contract. This ad hoc approach to due diligence may no longer be appropriate or reasonable in the context of licensing large, extremely sensitive databases.

To help ensure proper documentation and uniformity of the due diligence process, especially for high-risk arrangements involving the licensing or access to large databases, businesses should consider developing a standard due diligence questionnaire for relevant third parties to complete. Areas covered by the questionnaire would include corporate responsibility, insurance coverage, financial condition, personnel practices, information security policies, physical security, logistical security, disaster recovery and business continuity, and other relevant issues.

Use of a standardized questionnaire has a number of significant benefits:

- It provides a uniform, ready-made framework for due diligence.
- It ensures an "apples-to-apples" comparison of responses (e.g., in the context of a request for proposals [RFP] process).
- It ensures that all key areas of diligence are addressed and that none are overlooked.
- It provides an easy means of incorporating the due diligence information directly into the parties' contract. That is, the completed questionnaire can be attached as an exhibit to the final agreement between the parties.
- It places the third party on notice from the outset that information security is a key consideration.

From the outset, third parties must be on notice that the information they provide as part of the due diligence process and, in particular, in response to the due diligence questionnaire, will be relied on when deciding to move forward with the relationship and that the response will be incorporated into any final agreement between the parties. To be most effective, the questionnaire should be presented to third parties at the earliest possible stage in the relationship. It should be included as part of all relevant RFP or, if no RFP is issued, as a stand-alone document during preliminary discussions with the third party.

Key areas for the due diligence questionnaire include the following:

- Information security in general:
  - Does the third party have an established policy to ensure that potential or actual security incidents are promptly reported to the relevant company personnel?
  - Does the third party have a written information security policy? How often is the policy reviewed and updated? When was the last update?
  - Has the third party conducted a recent Statement on Standards for Attestation Engagements (SSAE) 16 (the successor to the SAS 70 audit; for more information, see www.aicpa.org)? Were any deficiencies corrected? Is a copy of the audit report available for review? How often does the third party conduct audits? Has the audit report identified any material issues that require remediation? If so, have the issues been resolved? Is the resolution documented?
  - Does the third party have a policy controlling transfer of highly sensitive information to removable media (e.g., USB fobs, CDs, and other similar devices and storage media)?
- The third party's financial condition:
  - Is the third party a private or public company?
  - Can the business obtain copies of the most recent financial statements? Financial condition may not appear to be a critical factor for information security purposes, but the possibility that the third party may file bankruptcy or simply cease to do business while in possession of the most sensitive information of a business presents a substantial risk, especially in today's current economic environment. In such instances, it may be difficult, if not impossible, to retrieve the data and ensure it has been properly scrubbed from the third party's information systems.
- Insurance coverages:
  - What types of coverage does the third party have?
  - What are the coverage limits and other terms?
  - Are the coverages "claims made" or "occurrence" based?
  - Does the third party's insurance cover liability related to security breaches? Hacking and other computer crimes?

- Corporate responsibility:
  - Are there, for example, any criminal convictions, recent material litigation, or instances in which the third party has had a substantial compromise of security or been investigated for privacy violations?
- Subcontractors:
  - Will the third party require the use of any subcontractors or affiliates in the performance of the agreement?
  - Will the third party use subcontractors or affiliates outside the country in which the business is based?
  - Where are the subcontractors and affiliates located?
  - What types of services will the subcontractors provide?
  - What information, if any, of the business will be sent to these entities? Transmission of data to contractors or subcontractors located outside the United States has been identified as creating unique risk. Such entities will not be subject to the jurisdiction of courts in the United States. In addition, the laws of the other jurisdictions may not provide nearly the level of protection offered in the United States. Some countries are notorious for not respecting the intellectual property and privacy rights of others. It would be critical to know if the third party intends to transfer the intellectual property of a business to those jurisdictions.
- Organizational security procedures:
  - What are the third party's information-handling policies?
  - Does it have a dedicated information security team?
  - Is there an incident response team? How is it documented?
  - What are the third party's information security practices with contractors and agents (e.g., due diligence, requisite nondisclosure agreements, specific contractual obligations relating to information security)?
- Physical security:
  - What physical security measures and procedures does the third party employ?
  - Is the facility fenced? Are ingress and egress points monitored? Are surveillance cameras used? Are employees permitted to bring backpacks, briefcases, smartphones with cameras, recording devices, writing materials, and the like into the areas of the third party's facilities where highly sensitive information is handled?

- Encryption:
  - Does the third party use encryption to protect sensitive information?
  - How is encryption used? Data "at rest," "data in motion," and so on? That is, is the data only encrypted when stored but not in transit over internal and external networks?
  - Are the third party's internal wireless networks secured with strong encryption? There are numerous instances in which third-party Wi-Fi networks have been hacked because they are either entirely unsecured or use easily breached security measures.
  - Is the method of encryption consistent with the appropriate standards (e.g., guidances from the National Institute of Standards and Technology [NIST])?
- Destruction and retention:
  - Does the third party destroy media containing sensitive information through appropriate methods, such as shredding paper, film, or other hard copies and clearing, purging, or otherwise irretrievably destroying electronic media in accordance with relevant industry standards (e.g., the Department of Defense [DoD] 5220-22-M Standard (available at www.dtic.mil) or NIST Special Publication 800-88, *Guidelines for Media Sanitization* (available at www.csrc.nist.gov))?
  - Does the third party have retention policies that permit it to retain customer intellectual property after it is no longer needed for the engagement in which it was disclosed? How long will the information be retained? What, if any, uses can the third party make of the intellectual property? What measures will be used to ensure the intellectual property continues to be protected? In most instances, if the third party must retain the intellectual property, all relevant information security, confidentiality, indemnity, and so on provisions of the agreement should continue to apply for as long as the third party retains the information.
- Technological security:
  - Does the third party have appropriate access controls and logging/audit trail capabilities?
  - Does the third party use system access control on its systems to limit information access to only those of its personnel who are specifically authorized?
- Policies:
  - Does the third party have an information security policy and privacy policy?

- What is the revision history of its policies?
- Are there any instances for which the third party has had to report a significant breach of security?
- Contingency plans:
  - What are the third party's business continuity/disaster recovery plans? When was its last test? When was it last audited, and were there any adverse findings in the audit? Have deficiencies been corrected?
  - What is the revision history of its plan?
  - What security procedures are followed at the recovery site? The recovery site should ensure data is protected to the same extent as the primary site where services will be performed.
- Special issues for software developers:
  - If the third party is a software developer, what are its development and maintenance procedures?
  - What security controls are used during the development life cycle?
  - Does the third party conduct security testing of its software?
  - Does the third party maintain separate environments for testing and production?
  - Does the third party license code from third parties for incorporation into its products, and if so, what types of code?

3.4 THE SECOND TOOL: KEY CONTRACTUAL PROTECTIONS

Most contracts have little or no specific language governing information security. At most, there is a passing reference to undefined security requirements and a basic confidentiality clause. Today's best practices relating to the protection of data suggest that far more specific language is required.

In addition to an appropriately written license grant (see Chapter 7, "Licensing Big Data"), the following protections related to information security should be considered for inclusion in relevant agreements:

- Warranties
- Specific information security obligations
- Indemnity

- Responsibility for costs associated with security breach notification
- Limitation of liability
- Confidentiality
- Audit rights

3.4.1 Warranties

In addition to any standard warranties relating to how the agreement is to be performed and authority to enter into the agreement, the following specific warranties relating to information security should be considered in appropriate agreements:

- A warranty requiring the third party to comply with "best industry practices relating to information security." This creates an evolving standard to keep pace with advances in the industry as security measures improve over time.
- A warranty against sending data and intellectual property offshore to subcontractors or affiliates unless specifically authorized to do so by the customer.
- If a due diligence questionnaire has been completed, a warranty stating that the responses to the due diligence questionnaire (described previously) are true and correct. The questionnaire should be attached as an exhibit to the contract.
- To the extent any data disclosed is subject to a state or federal law or regulation (personally identifiable information), a warranty of compliance with those laws and regulations.

3.4.2 Specific Information Security Obligations

In addition to the general information security warranty discussed and confidentiality clause, consider addressing information that is more specific on security obligations. Where appropriate, insert specific language requiring the third party to secure and defend its information systems and facilities from unauthorized access or intrusion, to participate in joint security audits, to periodically test its systems and facilities for vulnerabilities, to use appropriate encryption and access control technology, and to use proper methods and techniques for destruction of sensitive information (e.g., the DoD 5220-22-M Standard or NIST Special Publication 800-88, *Guidelines for Media Sanitization*).

3.4.3 Indemnity

In addition to general indemnity language, a specific provision requiring the third party to hold the business harmless from claims, damages, liabilities, and expenses incurred as a result of a breach of the security obligations should be included. That is, the third party should protect the business from lawsuits and other claims that result from the third party's failure to adequately secure its systems.

3.4.4 Limitation of Liability

Most commercial agreements have some form of "limitation of liability"—a provision designed to limit the type and extent of damages to which the contracting parties may be exposed. It is not uncommon to see these provisions disclaim a party's liability for all consequential damages (e.g., lost profits, harm to the reputation of the business) and limit all other liability to some fraction of the fees paid. These types of provisions are almost impossible to remove, but it is possible to require certain exclusions for damages, including damages flowing from a breach of the confidentiality or information security obligations. Without these exclusions, the contractual protections described previously would be largely illusory. If the third party has no real liability for breach of privacy or confidentiality because the limitation of liability limits the damages the third party must pay to a negligible amount, the contractual protections of the business are rendered meaningless.

3.4.5 Confidentiality

A fully fleshed-out confidentiality clause should be the cornerstone for information security protections related to intellectual property and highly sensitive databases. The confidentiality clause should be drafted broadly to include all information the business desires to be held in confidence. Specific examples of protected information should be included (e.g., source code, proprietary care plans, marketing plans, new product information, trade secrets, financial information). Although the term of confidentiality protection is often fixed (e.g., five years from the date of disclosure or, more likely, termination of the agreement), ongoing, perpetual protection should be expressly provided for valuable information such as the trade secrets of the business or personally identifiable data.

Requirements stating that the business mark relevant information as "confidential" or "proprietary" should be avoided. These types of requirements are unrealistic in the context of most arrangements. The parties frequently neglect to comply with these requirements, resulting in proprietary, confidential information being placed at risk.

3.4.6 Audit Rights

The agreement should include clear rights permitting the business to audit the third party to confirm compliance with the terms of the agreement and applicable law, including the license grant for the database. While reasonable limitations can be included regarding the number of times that audits may be conducted and their timing, businesses should avoid any strict limitations (e.g., limiting audits to only once per year or imposing an excessive notice period before the audit can be conducted). The third party must reasonably cooperate with the audit, including providing all appropriate documentation. That cooperation should be at no cost to the business. Finally, the audit language should require that the third party furnish the business with copies of all relevant third-party audit reports (e.g., SSAE 16).

3.5 THE THIRD TOOL: AN INFORMATION SECURITY REQUIREMENTS EXHIBIT

The final tool in minimizing information security risks is a potential exhibit or statement of work that specifically defines the security requirements relevant for a particular engagement. For example, engagements in which highly sensitive information will be entrusted to a third party may require the third party to observe strict practices in its handling of the information; for example, the information security requirements exhibit may prohibit the third party from transmitting the information on the business over internal wireless networks (e.g., 802.11a/b/g) or from transferring that information to removable media that could be easily misplaced or lost. The exhibit may also contain specific requirements for use of encryption and access control technology, decommissioning hardware, and storage media on which the business's information was stored to ensure that the information is properly scrubbed from the hardware and media. Other specific physical and technological security measures should be identified as relevant to the particular transaction.

3.6 CONCLUSION

Unique risks are presented when Big Data is entrusted to third parties. Those risks can be mitigated by employing the tools discussed in this chapter: appropriate and uniform due diligence, use of specific contractual protections relating to information security, and, where relevant, use of exhibits or other attachments to the agreement detailing unique security requirements to be imposed on the third party. Doing so will ensure data is handled in a secure manner. The due diligence questionnaire will enable the business to ask the right questions and obtain critical information—before the contract is entered into—with respect to the ability of the third party to adequately safeguard intellectual property. The contractual provisions described (1) set out the business's expectations with respect to security requirements, (2) provide the basis for compelling the third party to comply with those requirements, and (3) give the business remedies for asserting a claim against the third party in the event of the third party's failure to provide adequate security measures. Finally, the optional information security requirements exhibit allows the business to customize security requirements to fit the particular circumstances of the engagement and provide a level of detail that ordinarily would not be found in standard contractual provisions.

4

Privacy and Big Data

Chanley T. Howell

4.1 INTRODUCTION

This chapter examines the privacy compliance challenges when dealing with Big Data and provides guidance on how to comply with applicable privacy laws, regulations, and standards when implementing Big Data initiatives. Big Data is different from structured data in terms of the privacy issues and challenges in protecting personal data. There are two fundamental characteristics of Big Data that make it different: (1) The analysis of Big Data is often for a purpose different from the original purpose for which the data was gathered, and (2) the volume of data used for Big Data purposes can be vastly greater than that found in traditional structured databases.

The primary objective of Big Data is to derive new insights—predicting outcomes and behavior based on very large volumes of data collected from a large number of sources. Each data source, in turn, typically contains data that relates to numerous data subjects. Thus, the gathering and analysis of the data for Big Data purposes is often different from the purpose for which the data was obtained at the time it was initially collected. This change in purpose regarding the use of the data creates issues under the principles of notice and choice, which are fundamental to privacy laws and standards.

Consumers should be given notice of how a company will use and share the consumer's personal information and be provided a meaningful choice with respect to such use and sharing. Any company collecting data must understand how it intends to use personal information when it is collected so that the required notice and choices can be provided. For example, an online retailer may collect large volumes of purchase and transaction histories for the primary purpose of documenting sales for revenue reporting and product purchases for warranty purposes. The retailer may also want to analyze that data to identify purchasing trends, thereby using that information for marketing purposes. If the retailer did not provide adequate notice to the customer of this subsequent Big Data use, it may run afoul of the notice and choice privacy principles.

The second characteristic of Big Data that makes it different from traditional structured data is the sheer volume of the data. Another core principle common to privacy laws and standards is access. The access principle provides that consumers are entitled to know what information a company collects about the consumers so they can effectively exercise their right to choose how that information is used. With a single database containing a manageable amount of customer information, this may not be too difficult. If, however, the dataset resides over multiple databases, and perhaps even with third-party data processors, providing the consumer with access, choice, and transparency can be difficult. Companies should design their Big Data initiatives on the front end with the ability to provide access, choice, and transparency to consumers by taking the steps identified in this chapter.

4.2 PRIVACY LAWS, REGULATIONS, AND PRINCIPLES THAT HAVE AN IMPACT ON BIG DATA

The United States does not have a comprehensive federal privacy regimen, such as the Data Protection Act of the European Union. Rather, privacy laws in the United States follow a sectoral approach (e.g., health care, financial, educational information). These sectoral laws are expanded by a layer of guidelines, principles, and rulings from the Federal Trade Commission (FTC). That is not the end of the privacy regulation. States have their own patchwork of privacy and security laws, covering a broad range of subjects, including the protection of health information, financial information, and more general personal information. Finally, all these federal and state laws are subject to a stream of court decisions that provide practical interpretations of the laws and additional compliance direction to data holders. As a result, navigating which of the multiple layers of laws applies to each type and source of data presents a significant compliance challenge for most organizations.

The layers of regulation can act independently and cumulatively, depending on factors such as the type of information collected, the age of the individual from whom the data is collected, and the manner of data collection. For example, at the federal level, financial information of various types is protected under the Fair Credit Reporting Act (as amended and supplemented by the Fair and Accurate Credit Transactions Act) and the Gramm-Leach-Bliley Act (GLBA). Health information is regulated under the Health Insurance Portability and Accountability Act (HIPAA; as amended and supplemented by the Health Information Technology for Economic and Clinical Health Act). Information collected from children under the age of 13 is regulated by the Children's Online Privacy Protection Act. Student information is protected under the Family Educational Rights and Privacy Act. The Telephone Consumer Protection Act, Telemarketing Sales Rule, and the Controlling the Assault of Non-Solicited Pornography and Marketing Act (CAN-SPAM) protect the privacy of consumers with respect to receiving marketing communications from companies. Finally, any gaps in the coverage of these laws are filled by various enforcement decrees, rulings, guidelines, and principles published by the FTC as well as court decisions interpreting both the statutes and the FTC's pronouncements. Because of this complexity, compliance efforts can be greatly enhanced by understanding the underpinnings of the privacy and security laws. The remainder of this chapter discusses the foundational principles of privacy compliance and key laws with which your organization's data collection and handling policies may need to comply.

4.3 THE FOUNDATIONS OF PRIVACY COMPLIANCE

Throughout this chapter, we discuss the importance of transparency with respect to Big Data initiatives and complying with privacy requirements. Transparency is the combination of notice, access, and choice. Together, notice, access, and choice underlie nearly all laws and regulations governing data privacy, and these principles must be understood and incorporated into effective policies governing data collection and use in your organization.

4.4 NOTICE

For over 20 years, notice has been at the core of essentially all global privacy laws, regulations, and principles. In 1998, the FTC presented its Online

Privacy report to Congress, which included the Fair Information Practice Principles (FIPPs). This report drew heavily from privacy principles in other jurisdictions, such as the Organization for Economic Cooperation and Development (OECD) Guidelines on the Protection of Privacy and Transborder Flows of Personal Data (1980) and the European Union Directive on the Protection of Personal Data (1995). As noted by the FTC, "the most fundamental principle is notice."[1] Although the content of the notice will vary based on the substantive practices of the organization, the FIPPs note that the following disclosures are critical to providing proper notice to consumers:

- The entity collecting the data.
- The uses to which the data will be put.
- Potential recipients of the data.
- The nature of the data collected and the means by which it is collected if not obvious (e.g., passively, by means of electronic monitoring, or actively, by asking the consumer to provide the information).
- Whether the provision of the requested data is voluntary or required and the consequences of a refusal to provide the requested information.
- The steps taken by the organization to ensure the confidentiality, integrity, and quality of the data.

4.5 CHOICE

As stated by the FTC in the FIPPs, "At its simplest, choice means giving consumers options as to how any personal information collected from them may be used."[2] Choice is particularly relevant with respect to secondary uses of information—using information in ways beyond those necessary to complete the contemplated transaction. For example, when ordering products online, the consumer understands his or her mailing address and credit card information are needed by the seller to process and fulfill the purchase. The individual would not, however, necessarily understand or appreciate that this information could be used by the company for future marketing communications or shared with third parties for their own direct marketing purposes. The choice principle states that the consumer is entitled to know when there will be secondary uses of personal information, and the consumer must be provided the right not to permit such uses.

Big Data collection and analytics make it more probable that information collected for one purpose will be used for another. For example, as reported in the *New York Times*, Target used shopping statistics to predict which women were pregnant and then marketed pregnancy products to them.[3] Target analyzed historical shopping data to identify changing trends in purchasing behaviors that could be associated with pregnancy. For example, the data revealed that women bought larger quantities of unscented lotion around the beginning of their second trimester, and during the first 20 weeks, pregnant women loaded up on supplements like calcium, magnesium, and zinc. According to the *New York Times* article, Target was able to identify about 25 products that could be used to develop a "pregnancy prediction" score, as well as the estimated due date. This enabled Target to send certain coupons directed not only to the fact of the pregnancy but also to the stage of the pregnancy.

According to the *New York Times* article, about a year after Target developed the pregnancy predictor model, an angry man complained to Target, demanding an explanation for why Target was sending his teenage daughter coupons for baby clothes and cribs. The manager apologized in person and then called the father a few days later to reiterate the apology. The embarrassed father told the manager: "I had a talk with my daughter," he said. "It turns out there's been some activities in my house I haven't been completely aware of. She's due in August. I owe you an apology."

Target did not face enforcement action, but did have to contend with the public relations fallout after the *New York Times* article went viral and ended up modifying its privacy policy. Target's current privacy policy is now much more informative about what information is collected and that it uses the information—including purchase history—for marketing purposes, such as to "deliver coupons, mobile coupons, newsletters, in-store receipt messages, emails, mobile messages, and social media notifications."[4] Target also permits its customers to opt out of receiving catalogs, coupons, and other marketing communications, as well as from Target sharing customer information with third parties for their own direct marketing purposes. The lesson learned from the Target example is that companies engaged in Big Data analytics using personal information for purposes other than those related to the original purpose for the collection of such data should be transparent regarding how the information is used and how the consumer can opt out of receiving marketing communications and sharing of personal information with third parties for marketing purposes.

Choice is typically obtained either through an opt-in or an opt-out presentation to the consumer. As discussed more fully in the following material, some laws with an impact on Big Data use are opt-in laws, while some are opt-out laws. Opt-in laws require affirmative action by the consumer to allow the collection and use of the information. Opting out permits the use of the information unless the consumer takes affirmative steps to prevent the collection and use of the information. Thus, for example, the Telephone Consumer Protection Act requires consumers to provide express written (opt-in) consent to receive telemarketing calls and text messages to cell phones before a company can make such calls or send text messages. The GLBA permits financial institutions to share personal information with third parties for marketing purposes unless the consumer opts out of such sharing by, for example, mailing in an opt-out form, opting out through an online form, or opting out by calling a toll-free telephone number. Similarly, the Federal Credit Reporting Act (FCRA) prohibits certain uses and sharing of personal information without proper notice and the opportunity to opt out of such uses and sharing. Under FCRA, consumers must be given the ability to opt out of disclosures to third parties or affiliates for marketing purposes or disclosure of credit report information to affiliates. As discussed in more detail in this chapter, companies engaging in Big Data initiatives need to be aware of laws that require choice and how those choices must be presented to consumers.

After-the-fact notice to the consumer without express consent can be ineffective. Accordingly, to avoid the need to renotify and obtain express consent from consumers, companies should anticipate, to the greatest extent possible, potential Big Data uses and provide proper notice for consumers when the information is first collected. Obtaining consent after the fact often results in large dropout or opt-out rates caused by consumers failing to provide the required consents.

4.6 ACCESS

Access is an individual's ability to (a) access data that a company has about the individual and (b) require the company to correct inaccurate information or delete information not needed or properly held by the company. Access is critical to ensuring personal information remains accurate and complete. To be effective, a consumer's ability to access relevant data must be timely and not overly burdensome with respect to cost or effort required to access the data. Similarly, the methods for reporting and challenging inaccurate information should be relatively quick and easy for the consumer to accomplish. Organizations should implement practices and procedures for updating, correcting, and deleting personal information as required by the consumer or applicable law.

The three principles—notice, choice, and access—are at the heart of a successful privacy compliance program for Big Data initiatives.

The following sections describe selected laws and legal requirements that often implicate privacy compliance for Big Data projects.

4.7 FAIR CREDIT REPORTING ACT

Companies can be subject to compliance with FCRA arising from the manner in which they collect, use, and share Big Data. FCRA regulates the sharing and use of personal information used for credit, insurance, employment, and certain other specified purposes. FCRA allows consumers to access their credit reports. This provides transparency to consumers so they can see what information the consumer reporting agencies have about them. In addition, if there are errors or inaccuracies in the information, the consumer can dispute the information and, if appropriate, require the consumer reporting agency to correct the information. It is commonly understood that the largest consumer reporting agencies (Experian, Equifax, and TransUnion) are consumer reporting agencies under FCRA. However, the reach of the act is not limited to the big three reporting agencies, and many more businesses than they may realize are subject to FCRA because of the way they use certain personal information.

Whether a company is a consumer reporting agency does not depend on how the company characterizes or markets itself, but rather the nature of the information it provides to third parties and the use of the information by third parties. A company is a consumer reporting agency if it provides "consumer reports" to third parties. Because of the increased regulatory obligations under FCRA and the increased risks resulting from noncompliance, many companies take steps to avoid that status. If a company is a consumer reporting agency, it is required to comply with the requirements of FCRA, such as the following:

- Provide consumer reports only to companies that agree to use them for a purpose that is permissible under FCRA (see discussion of permissible purposes further in the chapter).
- Obtain certification from users of consumer reports that the information will be used for permissible purposes under FCRA and only those purposes.
- Implement procedures to ensure the accuracy of information contained in consumer reports.
- Provide consumers with access to consumer reports, including sources of information and recipients of consumer reports on the consumer.
- Provide consumers with a Summary of Consumer Rights when making required privacy-related disclosures to the consumer.
- Take reasonable steps to verify the identity of third parties seeking disclosures from the consumer reporting agency.
- Correct inaccurate information contained in consumer reports.
- Reinvestigate information disputed by a consumer on notice from the consumer.

Complying with FCRA as a consumer reporting agency can be complex and burdensome. Failure to comply can result in state and federal regulatory actions, fines, and sanctions. Thus, businesses that use Big Data in a manner that requires compliance with FCRA as a consumer reporting agency should fully understand the compliance requirements, costs, and ramifications before doing so.

Companies receiving information that falls under the category of a consumer report are subject to compliance with FCRA as users of consumer reports. Compliance requirements include obtaining consent from consumers to obtain a consumer report (e.g., when the report will be used for employment purposes), using consumer reports only for purposes that are permissible under FCRA, and notifying consumers when adverse action has been taken (e.g., declining a loan) based on a consumer report.

4.8 CONSUMER REPORTS

FCRA goes further in its regulation of personal information than simply protecting the privacy of the information. Most privacy restrictions have to do with keeping personal information private, namely, not sharing it with third parties unless such sharing is permissible. FCRA goes further in regulating and restricting how the personal information—or in this case credit report information—can be used internally by a company for analytical and decision-making purposes.

The term *consumer report* is broad. The term includes information relating to a consumer's credit worthiness, character, general reputation, personal characteristics, or mode of living that is used (or expected to be used) in determining eligibility for credit or insurance or for employment purposes. FCRA limits uses of consumer reports to certain permissible uses. Permissible uses include issuing credit, evaluating a prospective employee, underwriting an insurance policy, and a catchall "legitimate business purpose" for transactions initiated by the consumer. To satisfy the legitimate business purpose, the information must be needed in connection with a business transaction initiated by the consumer or to determine whether the consumer continues to meet the terms of a transaction.

4.9 INCREASED SCRUTINY FROM THE FTC

Companies may frequently use Big Data in ways they do not fully realize or appreciate implicate FCRA compliance. Big Data use of personal information has recently resulted in increased attention from the FTC, demonstrating the importance of recognizing whether Big Data use triggers compliance with FCRA. In May 2013, the FTC conducted a sting operation uncovering ten companies that appeared to be selling personal information in violation of FCRA. The undercover FTC personnel acted as if they were interested in purchasing consumer information such as credit scores. The FTC made it clear to the companies that they intended to use the data for FCRA-covered purposes. They contacted 45 data brokers; 10 did not comply with FCRA requirements such as obtaining evidence from employers that the employee or prospective employee had been informed of and consented to the request.

Because the transactions were not completed, it is possible the data brokers would have complied with FCRA. However, the FTC was concerned that the ten companies expressed no intention of doing so. The companies appeared willing to provide the data without complying with

FCRA. The commission sent the companies informal warning letters, encouraging the companies to review their practices and procedures. This "warning shot over the bow" should be a warning to all companies that they should determine whether their Big Data uses implicate FCRA and, if so, ensure that the company takes appropriate action to comply.

Another example of increased FTC enforcement is in the area of rental histories, information that can be covered under FCRA. In April 2013, the FTC sent a letter to six companies that collected information about tenants' rental histories. These companies shared the information with prospective landlords who were considering renting to a certain tenant. The FTC took the position that if a company collects information about individuals' rental histories and provides this information to landlords for screening tenants, the company will be considered a consumer reporting agency and is required to comply with FCRA. As such, these companies would be required to notify landlords—as recipients and users of consumer reports—of their responsibilities. For example, if a landlord declines to rent based on the information provided by a company, the landlord has to notify the prospective tenant of that fact, give the consumer information about how to obtain a free copy of their report, and tell the consumer how to dispute information that is or may be inaccurate. Here, again, these companies likely did not realize their Big Data use of personal information required compliance under FCRA.

A third example of Big Data triggering FCRA compliance relates to use of information about employees. In an effort to fight employee theft, retailers throughout the United States have cooperated to create large databases of employees accused of theft. The retailers use the information for employment decisions, often having the effect of keeping the employee from working in the retail industry. The databases have been criticized for containing little verified information about suspected thefts and relating to situations that do not involve criminal charges.

Employees complained that the information may be used against them even though they did not actually engage in theft but merely were suspected of theft. In 2013, the FTC announced it would examine the legality of the employee theft databases in light of complaints it had received challenging the accuracy of the databases and the ability of employees or former employees to access the information and correct inaccurate information. The use of the information for employment purposes was deemed to be covered under FCRA, thereby triggering the compliance obligations and FTC oversight under FCRA.

4.10 IMPLICATIONS FOR BUSINESSES

These recent actions demonstrate that the FTC is on the lookout for companies using Big Data for FCRA purposes without complying with FCRA. Businesses looking to monetize their Big Data inventory by selling it or sharing it with third parties must therefore understand what triggers FCRA compliance. For example, selling or licensing information that enables companies to make credit or employment decisions triggers FCRA compliance. A business that sells information about a consumer to be used for determining whether to make a loan to such a consumer must comply with the requirements of FCRA. As discussed, if a business is required to comply with FCRA as a consumer reporting agency, it must comply with the FCRA requirements (e.g., providing consumer reports only for FCRA-permissible purposes; verifying permissible use from consumer report users; maintaining accuracy of the information; providing access to consumers; investigating consumer complaints; etc.). Although these additional regulatory burdens and risks may be consistent with the business model for Big Data use, they are factors that need to be considered when determining the feasibility of a Big Data initiative.

4.11 MONETIZING PERSONAL INFORMATION: ARE YOU A DATA BROKER?

Data brokers have recently come under the spotlight of the FTC. Data brokers aggregate information about individuals and sell the information to other businesses. Companies such as Acxiom, Lexis-Nexis, and Dun & Bradstreet are typically considered data brokers. But, it is not just the Big Data broker companies that are being looked at by the FTC. Rather, any business that desires to monetize the data it has about individuals by selling it or sharing it with third parties needs to be aware of the current regulatory environment.

The FTC is calling for legislation addressing access and transparency to address concerns about the growing data marketplace. Specifically, the FTC is calling for legislation requiring data brokers to create a centralized website where data brokers could (1) identify themselves to consumers and describe how they collect and use consumer data and (2) detail the access rights and other choices they provide with respect to the consumer data they maintain. Data brokers typically sell information for marketing purposes, rather than credit, employment or insurance underwriting purposes that would subject them to compliance under FCRA. In these circumstances, there is no comprehensive federal law directly requiring data brokers to provide consumers with access to the data they have collected about the consumers. As discussed, FCRA requires consumer reporting agencies to provide consumers with a copy of their credit report at no charge and permits consumers to correct and challenge inaccurate information. As long as the information provided by data brokers is not used for credit, insurance, employment, or other permissible purposes under FCRA, data brokers are not required to provide consumers with access to the information or the ability to correct inaccurate information.

Unlike a "consumer reporting agency" under FCRA, a "data broker" is not a defined term under applicable law. Essentially, a data broker is any company that collects personal information and discloses it to a third party for that third party's own use—typically marketing. It need not be the company's only line of business or even a primary line of business. Although a data broker typically "sells" the information for a fee, this is not necessary, particularly if the transfer is part of a larger business relationship between two parties. The key questions are whether the company is (1) collecting personal information and (2) disclosing it to a third party for that third party's own purposes. If the answer to both of those questions is yes, the company is a data broker.

4.12 THE FTC'S RECLAIM YOUR NAME INITIATIVE

The FTC has publicly expressed concern over the practices of some companies to adopt a "collect first, ask questions later" approach to personal information. From the FTC's perspective, this approach clearly runs contrary to the concepts of notice, access, choice, and transparency discussed. In an effort to address this disconnect, an initiative called Reclaim Your Name has been proposed at the FTC. Reclaim Your Name is intended to give consumers (1) the ability to find out how data brokers collect and use personal information, (2) access to information that data brokers have collected, (3) the ability to opt out if a data broker is selling information for marketing purposes, and (4) the opportunity to correct errors in information used for substantive decisions.

Sensitive data (such as that regarding health or credit card and other financial information) would require additional safeguards, such as "just-in-time" notifications and consent at the time the data is collected. Companies that participate in Reclaim Your Name agree to customize their information collection, use, notice, and choice mechanisms to the sensitivity of the information at issue. Thus, as the personal information becomes more sensitive (e.g., financial, health, and sexual orientation), the companies would provide greater transparency and more detailed notice and choice to consumers.

Reclaim Your Name also has an impact on the world of connected devices, such as utility meters, refrigerators, and personal medical devices, often called the Internet of Things. Connected devices often do not have a user interface. Consumers may not understand that the devices they are using are connected to the Internet and sending information to third parties. The FTC expects engineers and technologists to take the lead in seeing that these connected devices follow the privacy by design principles: collecting the minimum data necessary to make a device function properly and creating consumer-friendly tools and interfaces that explain the information being collected, the uses of the data, and who will have access to the data.

The Reclaim Your Name initiative is another example of the FTC's expectations with respect to privacy of personal information. Companies engaged in Big Data initiatives need to incorporate transparency, choice, and access principles into their initiatives following the compliance best practices described at the end of this chapter.

Acxiom Corporation, one of the largest data brokers, has taken action to get out in front with respect to transparency of data broker information. In September 2013, Acxiom introduced its About the Data (http://www. aboutthedata.com) website. The website allows consumers to access information that Acxiom has about the individual and that it provides to companies for marketing purposes. By using the site, consumers have the ability to correct the information that Acxiom has collected about them and can even opt out of allowing Acxiom to share the information with other companies for marketing purposes. Acxiom's actions in this area provide an example to other companies desiring to provide transparency in connection with their Big Data initiatives.

Undoubtedly, the FTC will continue to push for greater and greater transparency. Services such as Acxiom's About the Data website that provide additional transparency to consumers are likely to grow. Even outside the data broker industry, these developments demonstrate the importance of transparency in complying with applicable privacy laws and principles and satisfying the FTC's expectations. Companies will need to have the ability to provide consumers with readily available access to the information companies have about the individual, as well as the ability to correct or delete inaccurate information. This can be challenging, particularly with large datasets. If the information is being shared with third parties for marketing purposes, then the consumer should have the ability to opt out of that sharing.

4.13 DEIDENTIFICATION

Companies considering Big Data strategies should assess whether their goals can be accomplished with deidentified or anonymized data. Privacy laws do not apply to information and other data that have been deidentified, such that the information cannot be used, alone or in combination with other data, to identify an individual. For example, under HIPAA, information is sufficiently deidentified when "there is no reasonable basis to believe that the information can be used to identify an individual." As discussed more fully in Chapter 5 ("Federal and State Data Privacy Laws and their Implications for the Creation and Use of Health Information Databases"), this can be done through an expert determination or the "safe harbor" method.

The safe harbor method of deidentification of protected health information (PHI) requires that certain identifiers of the individual or of relatives, employers, or household members of the individual not be present in the dataset in question. The identifiers that must be removed include information such as name; dates (except the year) related to an individual, such as birth date, admission date, discharge date, and so on; telephone number; email address; Social Security number; and so on. If any of the "prohibited" identifiers are present in the dataset, then the information is not sufficiently deidentified. In addition, the data user must not have actual knowledge that the information could be used alone or in combination with other information to identify an individual who is a subject of the information.

Under the expert determination method, an expert must conclude that the information is sufficiently deidentified. A qualified expert is one with appropriate knowledge of and experience with generally accepted statistical and scientific principles and methods for rendering information not individually identifiable. The expert must determine that the risk is very small that the information could be used, alone or in combination with other reasonably available information, by a recipient to identify an individual who is a subject of the information.

Although HIPAA provides detailed requirements with respect to deidentification, most privacy laws (e.g., FCRA and GLBA) do not. Organizations concerned with deidentifying personal information regulated by laws that do not have deidentification guidelines should use the HIPAA standards as guidance for deidentifying the information.

Companies should exercise particular caution when relying on deidentification in connection with Big Data projects. Because of the enormous volumes of data that often come from multiple databases, the ability to reidentify data that an organization believes has been appropriately deidentified is greater in the context of Big Data. If the data is reidentified, or even reasonably capable of being reidentified, then the data has not been sufficiently deidentified and would remain subject to all applicable privacy laws, regulations, principles, and guidelines.

4.14 ONLINE BEHAVIORAL ADVERTISING

One of the most prevalent uses of Big Data is in the area of online behavioral advertising (OBA). Since the beginning of advertising, advertisers have desired to learn about customers and potential customers so they can identify individuals more likely to purchase their products, and they tailor their messaging to those more likely purchasers. In the online market, one way of doing this is to track users' website activities to build a profile of a user's characteristics and preferences.

OBA is defined by the Digital Advertising Alliance (DAA; discussed more fully further in this section) as the practice of collecting "data from a particular computer or device regarding web viewing behaviors over time and across non-Affiliate websites for the purpose of using such data to predict user preferences or interests to deliver advertising to that computer or device based on the preferences or interests inferred from such web viewing behaviors."[5] Using cookies and advertising networks, advertisers can track and profile users (or, more accurately, browsers) across multiple websites, log sites visited, links followed, and other online activity.

Using Big Data for OBA purposes can be done behind the scenes without the ordinary user realizing it is occurring. This, in turn, has resulted in consumer and privacy advocate complaints about secret tracking and spying on consumers, profiling them and using the information without their knowledge. Although little legislation has been passed in the OBA or "do-not-track" area, the business and advertising industries have responded by various self-regulatory efforts. The success or failure of these self-regulatory efforts have played and will continue to play a significant factor in whether legislation is ultimately passed and, if so, the parameters of the legislation.

OBA and do not track are clearly in the sights of the FTC. In its March 2012 report, *Protecting Consumer Privacy in an Era of Rapid Change*,[6] the FTC recognized the importance of developing an effective do-not-track regime. More recently, in an April 17, 2013, article, the *Los Angeles Times* reported that the FTC chairwoman had some tough words on do not track directed to the advertising industry. The chairwoman was quoted as saying, "Consumers still await an effective and functioning do-not-track system, which is now long overdue."[7] Online tracking is clearly on the FTC's radar.

Realizing the importance of effective self-regulation, the advertising industry has acted to develop an effective program for OBA and tracking. The most prominent program has been established by the DAA. This is a self-regulatory alliance for OBA standards and guidelines led by several advertising industry associations: American Association of Advertising Agencies, American Advertising Federation, Association of National Advertisers, Council for Better Business Bureaus (CBBB), Direct Marketing Association (DMA), Interactive Advertising Bureau, and Network Advertising Initiative.

The DAA principles require an easy-to-use choice option to give consumers the ability to conveniently opt out of some or all DAA participating companies' online behavioral ads if they choose. Participating companies can register to participate in the choice mechanism (http:// www.aboutads. info). The DAA principles address accountability and enforcement. Both the CBBB and the DMA play roles in ensuring compliance and enforcement of the DAA program. The CBBB and DMA utilize a monitoring technology platform to enforce accountability among participating companies with respect to the transparency and control requirements of the principles, as well as to manage consumer complaint resolution.

Companies using Big Data initiatives for OBA should comply with the DAA principles whether or not they choose to become DAA participating members. In the absence of OBA and do-not-track legislation, regulators and courts will look to self-regulatory programs such as the DAA program for guidance in determining industry standard practices for complying with commonly accepted privacy practices and principles.

4.15 BEST PRACTICES FOR ACHIEVING PRIVACY COMPLIANCE FOR BIG DATA INITIATIVES

The following are recommendations based on current best practices for achieving privacy compliance for Big Data initiatives:

- **Develop Data Flow Mapping**. Develop data flow mapping of personal information that will be collected from individuals or from third parties about the individuals (data mapping). See Figure 4.1 for an illustration of simple data flow mapping.
- The data mapping should identify the following:
  - The specific categories of personal information to be used in the initiative (e.g., name, address, telephone number, age, gender, etc.). The inventory should specifically identify the use of sensitive personal information, such as Social Security number, driver's license number, financial information (e.g., credit card and bank account information), health information, and information about sexual behavior or orientation.
  - How the personal information is collected (e.g., manually, electronically, online, etc.).
  - Where the data is stored (e.g., company servers, third-party data center).
  - In what applications the data is stored.
  - The purposes for and intended uses of the personal information.
  - Individuals within the organization who will need access to the personal information.
  - Third parties outside the organization to whom the personal information will be disclosed.

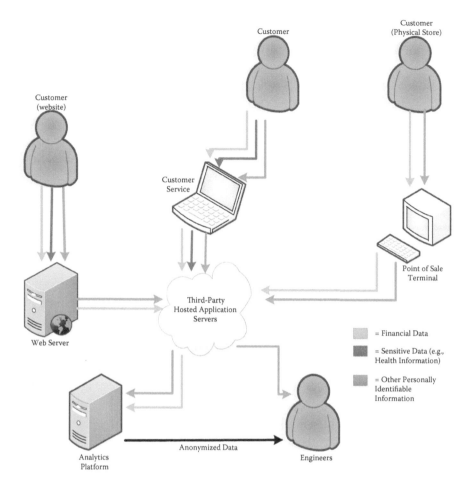

FIGURE 4.1
Data flow map.

- **Identify Applicable Sources of Legal Requirements.** With the information collected through the data mapping, the organization should be able to identify privacy laws, regulations, and self-regulatory standards applicable to the collection and use of the personal information. Potential sources of applicable legal requirements include the following:
  - Fair Credit Reporting Act and Fair and Accurate Credit Transactions Act (applicable to consumer reporting agencies and users of consumer report information)
  - GLBA (applicable to financial institutions)

- HIPAA (applicable to health care providers, health plans, and health care clearinghouses)
- Children's Online Privacy Protection Act (applicable to collection of personal information from children under the age of 13)
- Family Educational Rights and Privacy Act (applicable to student records and personal information)
- Consumer marketing laws (Telephone Consumer Protection Act, Telemarketing Sales Rule, CAN-SPAM)
- FTC's FIPPs

4.16 DATA FLOW MAPPING ILLUSTRATION

Data flow maps are tools that graphically represent what information comes into an organization, for what purposes that information is used, and who has access to that information. A data flow map will capture the results of a comprehensive data assessment (also known as a "data inventory" or "data audit") and present the results in a way that is easily consumable by the organization's strategic planning and compliance decision makers. Use of a data map can help ensure that an organization is in compliance with applicable law, the organization's privacy and information security policies, and contractual obligations.

Data flows can be represented in any graphical format suitable to the organization's needs. A simplified version of a data flow map showing information collected from customers may look like that presented in Figure 4.1:

- **Determine Methods for Complying with Applicable Legal Requirements**. Once the legal requirements have been identified, the organization can map out its strategies and methods for compliance. This effort may involve answering the following questions:
  - **Notice.** How will the company notify individuals of its personal information collection, use, and sharing practices? If the company receives personal information originally collected by a third party, how will the company confirm that the third party has the legal right to disclose the personal information to the company for the intended uses by the company?

- **Choice.** What choices must the company provide under applicable legal requirements, and what choices will the company voluntarily provide although not legally required? If applicable legal requirements mandate express or opt-in consent, how will the organization obtain that consent? If not legally required, will the organization obtain express consent to further mitigate its compliance risks? How will individuals exercise their choices?
- **Access.** How will the organization provide individuals with access to the personal information collected about them?
- **Accuracy.** How will the company verify and maintain the accuracy and completeness of the personal information?
- **Transfers to Third Parties.** Will the organization transfer any of the personal information to any third parties? If so, how will the organization achieve compliance with applicable legal requirements that may restrict the sharing of personal information?
- **Limiting Collection and Storage.** How will the company limit the amount of personal information collected to only that needed for the identified purposes? What practices and procedures will the company have in place to destroy the personal information when it is no longer needed for the identified purposes or as otherwise required by applicable legal requirements?
- **Security.** How will the organization comply with applicable legal requirements and industry standards with respect to security of the personal information? What practices and procedures will the organization have in place to respond to breaches of privacy or security?
- **Implement Compliance Program.** Once the company has mapped out the steps to be taken to achieve compliance, it can implement the program.
  - **Gap Identification.** The company should first identify gaps between its current practices and procedures as compared to the practices and procedures identified during the process described previously.
  - **Gap Remediation.** The organization should then remediate those gaps by determining how it will modify its business processes to align with the desired compliance requirements.
  - **Documentation.** The company should develop applicable policies, notices, and operating procedure documents based on the identified compliance requirements and gap remediation activities.

- **Education and Training.** The organization should then educate and train all applicable employee and contractor personnel with respect to the identified steps to achieve compliance.

NOTES

1. Privacy Online: A report to Congress, Federal Trade Commission, June 1998, 7.
2. Privacy Online: A report to Congress, Federal Trade Commission, June 1998, 8.
3. Charles Duhigg. How Companies Learn Your Secrets. *The New York Times*, February 16, 2012. http://www.nytimes.com/2012/02/19/magazine/shopping-habits.html.
4. Target Privacy Policy, Our marketing purposes, www.target.com/spot/privacy-policy
5. Self-Regulatory Principles for Online Behavioral Advertising, 2.
6. http://www.ftc.gov/sites/default/files/documents/reports/federal-trade-commission-report-protecting-consumer-privacy-era-rapid-change-recommendations/120326 privacyreport.pdf
7. Jessica Guynn. FTC Calls on Online Ad Industry to Agree on Do-Not-Track Standard. *Los Angeles Times*, April 17, 2013. http://articles.latimes.com/2013/apr/17/business/la-fi-tn-ftc-online-ad-industry-do-not-track-20130417.

5

Federal and State Data Privacy Laws and Their Implications for the Creation and Use of Health Information Databases

M. Leeann Habte

5.1 INTRODUCTION

Spurred by recent technological advances such as the proliferation of electronic medical records and mobile devices, the enhancements to computing platforms and infrastructure, and the development of new data-sharing and data-mining tools, there has been a dramatic increase in the ability of organizations to generate, aggregate, store, and analyze health information. Adding to the already sizable datasets maintained by individual health care organizations is relevant health data maintained by, among others, government agencies, mobile device companies, cloud services, social media, and collaborating hospitals, insurers, and physicians.

Secondary uses of these large datasets are creating unprecedented opportunities to drive innovation in health care. Industry experts, researchers, employers, payers, and providers are using Big Data to identify the most effective and cost-saving treatment protocols (e.g., comparative effectiveness research, patient monitoring, and decision support); improve products and services (e.g., predictive modeling for new drugs and personalized medicine); and improve public health surveillance and response. McKinsey & Company estimates that Big Data could be worth $9 billion to U.S. public health surveillance alone (by improving detection of, and response to, infectious disease outbreaks) and $300 billion to American health care in general.[1] Big Data is also creating new business models, such as cloud-based services and consumer applications (which generate valuable new data with potential secondary uses in the health care sector), and the aggregation and synthesis of health information to provide data and services to third parties. A 2013 evaluation of the marketplace by McKinsey & Company revealed that over 200 businesses created since 2010 are developing innovative tools to make use of available health care information.

5.2 CHAPTER OVERVIEW

Creation and use of Big Data in health care involves data obtained from multiple sources and of various types. For example, datasets may be built with clinical or claims data from health insurers or health care providers, combined with clinical or claims data released by government agencies, such as the Centers for Disease Control and Prevention (CDC) or the Centers for Medicare and Medicaid Services (CMS). Claims or clinical data may also be integrated with data obtained from consumers, for example, through personal health records (PHRs), mobile devices, and other consumer data (e.g., data captured from online browsing history, social media, or GPS systems). The value of this data is virtually limitless. Nevertheless, the ability to use this data is subject to multiple and overlapping layers of regulation. The object of this chapter is to provide you with an understanding of the web of regulation that has an impact on the use of health information and of how to minimize compliance issues arising from Big Data initiatives that use health information.

In the United States, the legal issues associated with the aggregation and uses of individually identifiable health information are complex because there are no overarching privacy principles that apply to all such information. Both federal and state regulations are largely sector specific. For example, the Health Insurance Portability and Accountability Act (HIPAA)[2] governs protected health information (PHI), which includes demographic, clinical, and financial information about an individual that is created or received by a covered entity.[3] The definition of PHI encompasses a broad range of information; however, HIPAA applies only to certain entities—health plans, health care clearinghouses, and certain health care providers that engage in standard electronic transactions. As a result, the regulatory protections afforded PHI are applicable only to information created or received by a limited group of actors defined as covered entities.

For example, HIPAA does not govern the health information in education records covered by the Family Educational Rights and Privacy Act (such as information generated in school health clinics); employment records held by a covered entity in its role as employer (such as records related to sick leave or records generated in an on-site health clinic); or information regarding a person who has been deceased for more than 50 years.[4] HIPAA also does not apply to the health information maintained in a personal health record (PHR) offered by an employer (separate from the employer's group health plan) or made available directly to an individual by a PHR vendor that is not a HIPAA covered entity. Nor does HIPAA govern health information gathered directly from consumers, such as information gathered through online applications.[5]

In addition to HIPAA, which may be the best-known law governing health information, there are other federal statutes that proscribe privacy protections, which may also apply to a covered entity. Such statutes include the federal confidentiality of substance abuse records statutes,[6] which protect patient records that are maintained by, or in connection with, a federally assisted drug or alcohol program, the Privacy Act of 1974,[7] which governs the privacy of information contained in a system of records maintained by a federal agency (or its contractors), and the federal Clinical Laboratory Improvement Amendments (CLIA),[8] which regulates disclosure by laboratories. In addition, the Gramm-Leach-Bliley Act[9] and, in some cases, the Employee Retirement Income Security Act[10] may apply to covered entity health plans.

Furthermore, while HIPAA provides a baseline for federal health information privacy protection, HIPAA does not preempt contrary state laws or regulations that are more stringent than HIPAA with respect to the protection of the privacy of health information.[11] The result is a patchwork of different standards for data privacy.

Although state laws that govern medical or health information vary markedly from state to state, there are certain generalities that can be made. A small group of states has comprehensive and relatively stringent privacy schemes that govern health or medical information. Almost all states have enacted laws that apply to specific categories of sensitive information, such as genetic information, HIV test results, substance abuse information, and mental health information. The determination of the legal requirements associated with health information is further impacted by the type of data, the source of data, and the state with jurisdiction over the data. Despite the intricacies involved in the analysis of these laws, such an analysis is an essential step to structuring a compliant Big Data initiative that includes health information.

The remainder of this chapter discusses the following:

- The key federal privacy issues pertaining to the collection and secondary use of health data collected from entities governed by HIPAA versus information collected from individuals.
- Key state law issues that have an impact on the collection and use of health data, including data ownership issues.

5.3 KEY CONSIDERATIONS RELATED TO SOURCES AND TYPES OF DATA

HIPAA is the key federal law that governs what is referred to as PHI.[12] HIPAA prohibits the use or disclosure of PHI without individual authorization, except in limited circumstances defined in the Privacy Rule. The HIPAA Privacy Rule also requires covered entities to make reasonable efforts to limit the PHI used, disclosed, or requested for any purpose other than direct treatment to the "minimum necessary" to accomplish the intended purpose of the use, disclosure, except in limited circumstances.[13] The Privacy Rule applies to covered entities and to the "business associates" of such covered entities, that is, any downstream subcontractors that provide financial, administrative, data transmission, and certain other services for or on behalf of covered entities or on behalf of the business associates to such covered entities. Organizations that store or transmit PHI such as electronic health record (EHR) vendors and health information exchanges are all considered business associates under these regulations.[14]

5.4 PHI COLLECTED FROM COVERED ENTITIES WITHOUT INDIVIDUAL AUTHORIZATION

5.4.1 Analysis for Covered Entities' Health Care Operations

There are several alternatives under HIPAA that allow for the sharing and aggregation of PHI without patient authorization. For example, two or more covered entities that participate in joint activities may share PHI about their patients to manage and benefit their joint operations as an organized health care arrangement (OHCA). To qualify as an OHCA, the legally separate covered entities must be clinically or operationally integrated and share PHI for the joint management and operation of the arrangement.[15] Also, they must hold themselves out to individuals as an integrated system and inform individuals that they will share PHI for their joint operations.[16] Members of an OHCA are permitted to disclose PHI to other covered entity participants for the joint health care operations[17] activities of the OHCA without entering into business associate agreements.

The HIPAA Privacy Rule also allows business associates to aggregate PHI from multiple covered entities or an OHCA for health care operations purposes[18] of the covered entities with whom they contract. For example, accountable care organizations ("ACOs") participating in the Medicare Shared Savings Program (MSSP) may permissibly aggregate and analyze data from multiple participants and providers, either in the capacity of business associates or covered entities, to improve health care quality and reduce costs. Such uses and disclosures, according to CMS, are considered "health care operations" purposes.[19] However, the HIPAA Privacy Rule does not permit the further use or disclosure of PHI by the business associate for secondary purposes unless the data are deidentified, as discussed next.

5.4.2 Creation and Use of Deidentified Data

Covered entities or business associates may deidentify PHI under the Privacy Rule; this approach permits unlimited secondary uses of information derived from PHI. There are two methods through which PHI may be deidentified under HIPAA: (1) the safe harbor method, which requires the removal of specified individual identifiers (described in the following material), as well as an absence of actual knowledge by the covered entity that the remaining information could be used alone or in combination with other information to identify the individual, and (2) the expert determination method, which involves a formal determination by a qualified expert.[20] The safe harbor method of deidentification of PHI requires removal of 18 identifiers of the individual or of relatives, employers, or household members of the individual, including names, all elements of dates (except year), and all geographic subdivisions except for the first three digits of a zip code where the geographic unit contains more than 20,000 people. In addition, the covered entity must not have actual knowledge that the information could be used alone or in combination with other information to identify an individual who is a subject of the information.[21]

Use of the expert determination method of deidentification requires that an expert (a person with appropriate knowledge of and experience with generally accepted statistical and scientific principles and methods for rendering information not individually identifiable) makes a determination and documents that the risk of reidentification is small.[22] In many cases, the expert determination method may be a better alternative to satisfy the deidentification standard because the current statistical methods allow for preservation of a greater number of data elements than under the safe harbor method. In particular, geographic data (e.g., zip codes) and dates (e.g., dates of service), which cannot be included in a dataset that is deidentified under the safe harbor method, may permissibly be included in a dataset that is deidentified under the expert determination method.

5.4.3 Strategies for Aggregation and Deidentification of PHI by Business Associates

To establish its ability to aggregate and deidentify PHI in compliance with HIPAA, a business associate should ensure that its business associate agreement addresses the following issues.

- The business associate agreement should expressly state that the business associate may aggregate PHI for the health care operations purposes of the covered entity (or OHCA if applicable). This is important because a business associate is not permitted to use or disclose PHI for purposes other than those permitted by its business associate agreement or required by law.[23] The aggregation of PHI for health care operations is a permissible use of data by business associates under HIPAA.[24] Therefore, a business associate may permissibly aggregate data to perform analysis for the health care operations of organizations that contribute data under a business associate agreement. For example, business associates that conduct analysis for ACOs may aggregate data from all the ACO participant members and their providers for the analysis.
- The business associate agreement should also expressly permit the business associate to deidentify the information.[25] Under HIPAA, a business associate can only make secondary uses of aggregated data

for purposes other than the health care operations of the covered entity if the business associate deidentifies the data or obtains patient authorization for such uses.[26] In many cases, obtaining patient authorization for proposed secondary uses may not be feasible. On deidentification of such information, the data are no longer considered PHI and thus not subject to HIPAA. The data may therefore be analyzed, disclosed, or sold by the business associate without restriction.

* Finally, the business associate agreement should exclude deidentified data from any provisions that relate to the covered entity's ownership of the data, or it should include an express transfer of ownership interest in deidentified data.

5.4.4 Marketing and Sale of PHI

The HIPAA Privacy Rule restricts a covered entity or its business associate from using PHI for "marketing" communications (i.e., communications about a product or service that encourage recipients of the communication to purchase or use the products or services) of a third party) if it receives direct or indirect payment for making such communications. Generally, if the communication is marketing, then the communication can occur only if the covered entity first obtains an individual's "authorization." This definition of marketing has certain exceptions for refill reminders, and for certain treatment or health care operations purposes, provided that no financial remuneration is received from a third party in exchange for making the communication. To the extent that a covered entity or business associate intends to use Big Data for marketing purposes, the strategy for collection and use should involve obtaining individual authorization that satisfies the requirements of HIPAA.

If a covered entity proposes to engage in a "sale of PHI" (i.e., an exchange of PHI for direct or indirect payment), individual authorization is required unless the sale falls within a regulatory exclusion for purposes such as public health, or research as long as the payment is a reasonable, cost-based fee to cover the cost to prepare and transmit the PHI.[27] If authorizations for sale of PHI are obtained from individuals, such authorizations must state that remuneration for the PHI is involved.[28] If PHI is properly "sold" to a third party pursuant to an authorization or permitted under one of the exceptions set forth previously, and the third party is not subject to HIPAA, there are no restrictions on how the third party may further use, disclose, or sell the data. However, if the third party is subject to HIPAA as a covered entity, then the third party must continue to abide by the HIPAA Privacy Rule's restrictions on use or disclosure of any PHI that it creates or receives. For example, if a dataset containing PHI is sold to a data analytics company with patient authorization, the data is no longer subject to HIPAA's restrictions because such companies are not covered entities that are governed by HIPAA. On the other hand, if PHI is sold with patient authorization to a health care provider, as a covered entity, the health care provider can still only use and disclose such PHI in accordance with HIPAA.

Although sale of identifiable PHI is prohibited under HIPAA without individual authorization, sale of deidentified data has been held to be permissible in the limited number of state court cases in which this legal issue has arisen. In one case, the state court upheld the defendant provider's motion to dismiss, ruling that the HIPAA Privacy Rule does not restrict the use or disclosure of deidentified information because it is not PHI.[29]

5.4.5 Creation of Research Databases for Future Research Uses of PHI

Research databases often include clinical information or claims information that was created and maintained by covered entities that are subject to the HIPAA Privacy Rule. The Privacy Rule provides several key "pathways" that permit use of PHI to create research[30] databases for future research purposes:

- Collection and use of a limited dataset (which may include geographic information other than street address, all elements of dates and ages, and certain other unique identifying characteristics or codes). A covered entity may release a limited dataset if the researcher signs a data use agreement (DUA), which assures the covered entity that the recipient will protect the limited dataset and will not make any effort to reidentify individuals using the dataset.[31]
- Collection and use of deidentified data (discussed previously).[32]
- Pursuant to an institutional review board (IRB) or privacy board waiver of authorization. An IRB operating under a federal-wide assurance or a privacy board that functions under the Privacy Rule may grant a waiver or alteration of written authorization if the proposed use or disclosure will pose minimal risk to participants' privacy, the research could not practically be conducted without the

waiver or alteration of authorization and cannot be conducted using deidentified information, and other specified criteria are met.[33]

- With authorization from an individual to create the research repository.[34] According to Department of Health and Human Services (HHS), the development of research repositories and databases for future research purposes is itself a "research activity," thereby requiring authorization or waiver of authorization (discussed in the preceding item) to the extent PHI would be involved.[35]

Table 5.1 illustrates the advantages and disadvantages of these approaches.

Prior to the recent enactment of the Omnibus HIPAA Final Rule, the HIPAA Privacy Rule did not allow covered entities to use or disclose PHI for the creation of research databases of PHI for future unspecified research. Instead, the law required individual authorizations for each specific study. To facilitate secondary research activities using databases or data repositories, the HHS recently reversed this policy.[36] The revised HIPAA Privacy Rule allows covered entities to obtain individual authorization for the uses and disclosures of PHI for future research purposes as long as the authorization adequately describes the future research such that it would be reasonable for the individual to expect that his or her PHI could be used or disclosed for future research purposes.[37] The revised Privacy Rule also provides considerable flexibility regarding the (1) description of the PHI to be used and (2) description of the recipients of the PHI (perhaps unknown) for the future research.[38]

Much of the biomedical and behavioral research conducted in the United States is also governed either by the Federal Policy for the Protection of Human Subjects (also known as the Common Rule)[39] or the Food and Drug Administration's (FDA's) Protection of Human Subjects Regulations.[40] These human subjects regulations apply to federally funded and some private research activities.[41] Similar to the revised HIPAA requirement, these federal human subjects protection regulations require informed consent of the research participant for the creation of research databases and repositories; informed consent documents must, among other requirements, include an "explanation of the purposes of the research."[42] This requirement has been interpreted to permit researchers to collect specimens and data for future research whose specific purposes may be unknown. For example, the National Cancer Institute informs potential participants that their tissue may be used in all types of research, such as finding the causes of disease, developing new tests or new drugs,

TABLE 5.1
HIPAA Pathways for Research Databases

	Limited Dataset with DUA	Deidentified Dataset	Waiver of Authorization	Authorization/Consent
Advantages	No subject authorization or consent required. May be useful for health services, research, and related studies.	No subject authorization or consent required. Unlimited uses and disclosures permitted for any purpose. May commercialize data or results of analysis.	No subject authorization or consent required.	Requires interaction with the individuals who are the subject of the information.
Disadvantages	DUA may restrict further uses and disclosures, the length of time for data availability, and the ability to link with other datasets. Limited dataset includes only a few more elements than deidentified data, so its research uses may be limited.	Deidentification of data limits its research uses and is not useful for certain clinical studies.	Requires involvement of IRB or privacy board. IRB or privacy board may not approve if it would be feasible to request authorization from the individuals who are the subject of information.	May permit use for future unspecified research and commercialization of research results. HIPAA minimum necessary standard does not apply.

and genetic research, and that they have no right to decide the type of research in which their tissue is used.[43]

Although federal human subjects protections do not directly govern private research databases, they regulate the activities of researchers who may ultimately use the research repository to conduct particular studies. If informed consent was not obtained, the use of such data by federally funded research studies could be compromised. To optimize the value of private research databases to researchers and to ensure maximum flexibility of use for future research, informed consent for creation of the database and future research uses should be requested in concert with the request for authorization under HIPAA.

5.4.6 Sensitive Information

The HIPAA Privacy Rule also contains specific restrictions on the disclosure of PHI that is genetic information for underwriting and related purposes by covered health plans, which is described in Chapters 4 ("Privacy and Big Data") and 9 ("The Impact of Big Data on Insureds, Insurance Coverage, and Insurers"). Disclosure of psychotherapy notes is not permitted without specific and separate authorization from the individual who is the subject of the information.[44]

5.5 BIG DATA COLLECTED FROM INDIVIDUALS

5.5.1 Personal Health Records

Although HIPAA and the Health Information Technology for Economic and Clinical Health Act (HITECH Act) have increased the restrictions on the use and disclosure of PHI, the increased ability of health care organizations to effectively and efficiently aggregate patient health records obtained directly from patients is acting to mitigate the impacts of the HIPAA restrictions. For example, even though a PHR offered to a patient by a vendor (such as Microsoft Health Vault or WebMD Health Manager) may contain the same information as a PHR offered by a covered health care provider (such as a hospital that provides a patient portal to a PHR), the PHR provided by the vendor is not subject to the same legal requirements because the PHR vendor is not a covered entity that is governed by HIPAA.

In general, a PHR is an electronic record of an individual's health information by which the individual controls access to the information and may have the ability to manage, track, and participate in his or her own health care. HHS clarifies that the HIPAA Privacy Rule applies solely to PHRs that are offered by health plans or health care providers that are covered by the HIPAA Privacy Rule but not to those offered by employers (separate from the employer's group health plan) or by PHR vendors directly to an individual.

PHR vendors are governed by the privacy policies of the entity that offers them and subject to the jurisdiction of the Federal Trade Commission (FTC).[45] FTC regulations have established health breach-reporting obligations and applied these requirements to PHR vendors (online services that allow consumers to organize and store medical information from many sources), PHR-related entities that offer products through the vendor's website or access or send information to a PHR (such as web-based applications that allow patients to upload a reading from a blood pressure pedometer into a PHR), or third-party service providers to vendors of PHRs. The FTC treats violation of the breach-reporting regulation as an unfair or deceptive act or practice.[46]

Even though HIPAA does not directly regulate PHR vendors, PHR-related entities, or third-party service providers, the HIPAA Privacy Rule does regulate the disclosure of an individual's PHI by a HIPAA covered entity to such entities. Therefore, in cases where the PHR is populated by a covered entity, a HIPAA-compliant authorization from the individual who is the subject of the information must be obtained. Typically, a PHR vendor, PHR-related entity, or third-party service provider will request such authorization as part of the patient's registration for the services. The authorization may be executed electronically, provided any electronic signature obtained from the individual complies with applicable law.[47] Alternatively, a covered entity may provide the record to the individual for the individual to enter into his or her PHR.[48]

5.5.2 Mobile Technologies and Web-Based Applications

If data is gathered from consumers through a web-based application or mobile device that does not interface with a PHR, the information is outside the scope of both HIPAA and the FTC breach-reporting regulations. To address this and other gaps in privacy regulations, in 2014 the FTC plans to hold a series of forums to address privacy issues related to

(a) mobile device tracking (tracking consumers in retail and other businesses using signals from their mobile devices); (b) alternative scoring products (using predictive scoring to determine consumers' access to products and offers); and (c) consumer-generated and controlled health data (information provided by consumers to non-HIPAA-covered websites, health applications, and devices).[49] Consumer-generated and controlled health data include that on websites such as Patients Like Me, which allows patients to connect with other patients with a similar health condition and track their health and fitness; mobile devices, such as applications for asthmatics to track inhaler use; and many others. Absent a change in the law, these data are governed only by the privacy policy of the business and applicable state law.

In addition to the wealth of new health data generated by health applications and devices, the increased use of social networking tools such as Facebook, mobile tracking devices, and applications that put personal information in the public domain provide greater analytic capacity with fewer regulatory protections. Routine Big Data analytical techniques can now effectively assemble personal data that is not protected by any of the laws currently in effect. A well-known illustration of this is the way Target creatively collated scattered pieces of data about an individual's changes in shopping habits to predict the delivery date of pregnant shoppers—so that they could then be targeted with relevant advertisements through the use of "predictive analytics." Target's actions drew public attention when it sent coupons to a teenage girl, whose father did not know she was pregnant. Although Target did not stop using predictive modeling techniques, it did alter its advertising strategy to this target audience.[50] As this example illustrates, when businesses that are not subject to health data laws create or maintain sensitive health information, its privacy policy and practices for use of Big Data should reflect thoughtful consideration of the consumer's expectations.

5.5.3 Conclusion

PHR vendors, related entities, and other web-based applications should ensure that the individual reads and agrees to their privacy policies, which establish their uses and disclosures of individual health records and related personally identifiable information. If health information is collected directly from individuals for future research purposes, the entity should consider obtaining informed consent from the individual to enhance the viability of future research uses of the data.

5.6 STATE LAWS LIMITING FURTHER DISCLOSURES OF HEALTH INFORMATION

5.6.1 State Law Restrictions Generally

State laws that protect the confidentiality of health information have been labeled a "patchwork quilt" of privacy protection.[51] State laws vary with respect to the entities that they govern, the extent of the privacy protections, and the types of information that they address. Because of these differences, businesses that operate in multiple states often must comply with conflicting state regulations. There are several key issues that must be considered. First, state privacy laws apply to different entities than HIPAA. This means that an entity that is not regulated by HIPAA may still be subject to state privacy laws with respect to the individually identifiable health information that it maintains. Second, unlike HIPAA, certain state laws could affect the ability to do one or more of the following without individual consent: disclose individually identifiable health information for purposes other than treatment, use health information for research, or make any secondary use of certain sensitive information. In addition, state law may vest individuals with ownership rights in certain health information, such as genetic information. Certain states also impose specific requirements for valid individual authorizations for the use and disclosure of health information.

To illustrate these issues, we analyzed the privacy laws in ten states: Arizona, California, Florida, Georgia, New York, Massachusetts, Minnesota, Texas, Washington, and Wisconsin. In Table 5.2, we provide illustrative examples of more stringent laws in select states that demonstrate the ways state law has a potential impact on the creation of Big Data related to health.

The descriptions illustrate some of the more stringent state laws that require special consideration.[52] For example, California is unique in that it deems "any business organized for the purpose of maintaining medical information" to make such information available to an individual (for the purposes of managing his or her own health care) or to a provider of

TABLE 5.2

State Laws that Restrict Secondary Uses of Big Health Data

State	Privacy Laws
Arizona	**Sensitive Information** Requires specific authorization for any redisclosure of HIV information, which must be accompanied by a written statement and restricts redisclosure (Ariz. Rev. Stat. § 36-664.F). Limits redisclosure of HIV and communicable disease information obtained from health care providers (see also Ariz. Rev. Stat. § 36-664.A).
California	**Applicability** Applies to certain businesses that maintain medical information, as well as providers of health care, health care service plans, and contractors (Cal. Civil Code § 56.06, § 56.10). Includes very restrictive employer-related provisions that prohibit use and disclosure of employee health information (Cal. Civil Code § 56.20). Restricts disclosure of medical information by third-party administrators except in connection with administration of the program as required by law or with an authorization (Cal. Civil Code § 56.26). **Research** Prohibits researchers from redisclosing information received from regulated entities in a manner that identifies the patient (Cal. Civil Code § 56.10(c)(7)). Requires IRB review of research on mental health information governed by the Lanterman-Petris-Short Act and requires researchers to sign an oath to protect the confidentiality of subjects (Cal. Welf. & Inst. Code § 5328(e)). **Marketing and Sale of PHI** *Additional restrictions on "marketing communications."* Providers of health care, health care service plans, contractors, and corporations and their subsidiaries and affiliates are prohibited from intentionally sharing, selling, using for marketing, or otherwise utilizing medical information for purposes not necessary to provide health care services to a patient without patient authorization. (Cal. Civil Code § 56.10(d)) CMIA's exclusions from the definition of marketing are more limited than HIPAA; however, they only pertain to communications (1) for which the communicator does not receive direct or indirect remuneration from a third party; (2) made to current health plan enrollees informing them of their benefits and plan procedures, including the availability of more cost-effective drugs; (3) concerning "disease management programs" for chronic and seriously debilitating or life-threatening conditions, provided that notification of third-party remuneration is provided and patients are provided the opportunity to opt out of receiving future remunerated communications (Cal. Civil Code § 56.05). The definition of disease management programs is detailed and could be narrowly construed.

Continued

TABLE 5.2 (*Continued*)

State Laws that Restrict Secondary Uses of Big Health Data

State	Privacy Laws

Sensitive Information

Limits disclosure of HIV test results without individual authorization. The portion of the medical record that contains HIV test result information cannot be disclosed without special authorization (Cal. Health & Safety Code § 120975-121023). Limits release of information about psychotherapy visits without individual authorization (Cal. Civil Code § 56.104). Applies special protections to records of substance abuse programs that are facilities that are regulated by the department, such as outpatient methadone treatment programs. Prohibits further disclosure of information unless the consent expressly permits such disclosure (Cal. Health & Safety Code § 11845.5).

Authorization

Specific requirements for valid authorization. Authorization requirements are generally consistent with HIPAA, except they require patient authorization forms to be a typeface that is no smaller than 14-point type (Cal. Civil Code § 56.11).

Minnesota   **Applicability**

Minnesota's laws apply only to health care providers in Minnesota but are among the most restrictive in the country. Disclosure without authorization is generally permitted only to other health care providers, licensed facilities, and in medical emergencies (Minn. Stat. § 144.293).

Research

Limits release of health records to an external researcher solely for purposes of medical or scientific research and only as follows: "(1) Health records generated before January 1, 1997, may be released if the patient has not objected or does not elect to object after that date; (2) For health records generated on or after January 1, 1997, the provider must: (i) disclose in writing to patients currently being treated by the provider that health records, regardless of when generated, may be released and that the patient may object, in which case the records will not be released; and (ii) use reasonable efforts to obtain the patient's written general authorization that describes the release of records in item (i), which does not expire but may be revoked or limited in writing at any time by the patient or the patient's authorized representative. Authorization may be established if an authorization is mailed at least two times to the patient's last known address with a postage prepaid return envelope and a conspicuous notice that the patient's medical records may be released if the patient does not object, and at least 60 days have expired since the second notice was sent.

TABLE 5.2 (*Continued*)

State Laws that Restrict Secondary Uses of Big Health Data

State	Privacy Laws
	The statute includes further obligations that the provider make reasonable efforts to determine (1) that the use or disclosure does not violate any limitations under which the record was collected; (2) that the use or disclosure in individually identifiable form is necessary to accomplish the research or statistical purpose for which the use or disclosure is to be made; (3) that the recipient has established and maintains adequate safeguards to protect the records from unauthorized disclosure; and (4) that further use or release of the records in individually identifiable form to anyone (other than the patient) without the patient's consent is prohibited (Minn. Stat. § 144.295).

health care (for the diagnosis or treatment of an individual) as a "provider of health care" with regard to the confidentiality standards established in the Confidentiality of Information (CMIA).[53] The law applies to "medical information." The term *medical information* means any "individually identifiable" information regarding a patient's medical history, mental or physical condition, or treatment.[54] The *primary* purpose of the business need not be the maintenance of medical information; it merely has to be one of the purposes of the business. Therefore, arguably, this law has broad applicability to PHR vendors and other businesses with web-based consumer-facing applications. This law requires special consideration by any entities to whom this law would apply; although collection of data from individuals would be subject to lesser regulation under federal law, state law does not provide such a distinction.

State laws that govern the use of disclosure of individually identifiable health information for research generally fall into two categories: (1) Some states, such as Minnesota, do not allow disclosure unless the researcher makes reasonable attempts to obtain patient authorization; (2) other states, such as California, extend the requirements of the Common Rule for IRB oversight of research to private research that involves certain mental health records. However, these examples indicate that state law should be given careful consideration in any design of a research database or repository.

In California, the use of "medical information" for marketing without individual authorization is also regulated more stringently than other federal law. If a regulated entity under CMIA will receive remuneration from a third party (such as a drug or device manufacturer), it should obtain legal review of its proposed strategy for use of the information.

State laws also restrict the initial disclosure of individually identifiable health information and any redisclosure of such sensitive information. In some states, such as California and Arizona, specific authorization is required for the disclosure of information such as HIV test results, communicable disease, substance abuse information, or mental health information. Some states such as Arizona also restrict redisclosure of communicable disease and HIV information if it is obtained from health care providers. Therefore, a strategy for use of sensitive information should involve analysis of the restrictions that apply to such information and whether they vary, depending on the source of the information.

Finally, California is also one of the few states that regulates the form of a valid individual authorization. The CMIA authorization requirements are consistent with HIPAA, except they require that patient authorization forms be a typeface that is no smaller than a 14-point font.[55] Therefore, to the extent that a business that maintains medical information, such as a web-based consumer-facing application, must obtain individual authorization for its proposed uses of medical information, such authorization form should be designed to comply with these state-law-specific requirements.

5.6.2 Genetic Data: Informed Consent and Data Ownership

In any data collection or use strategy that involves genetic information, state law requires special consideration. Most states have genetic privacy laws, and such laws are generally more stringent than HIPAA and are not pre-empted. State genetic privacy laws typically require an individual's specific written consent for the collection, retention, use, or disclosure of genetic information about an individual, with certain exceptions, (i.e., when the use or disclosure of genetic information is necessary to a criminal investigation, necessary to comply with a court order, or in connection with anonymous medical research). In most cases, the state laws governing use and disclosure of genetic information apply to persons generally, although uses of genetic information by employers and insurers are further restricted.

Even though most state statutes have not addressed ownership of tissue samples to date, Florida and Georgia have established an individual's ownership of "genetic information" (Table 5.3). These statutes have not been tested to examine their validity or scope, but they suggest that any

TABLE 5.3

Select Genetic Privacy Laws

State	Privacy Laws
Arizona	**General Restriction on Disclosure** Results of a genetic test are privileged and confidential and may not be released to any party without the express consent of the subject. There is an exception for medical research or public research conducted pursuant to applicable federal or state laws and regulations governing clinical and biological research or if the identity of the individual providing the sample is not disclosed to the person collecting and conducting the research (Ariz. Rev. Stat. Ann. § 12.2802). Arizona state provides an example of an authorization form that permits disclosure of the results of a genetic test (http://www.azinsurance.gov/bulletin/97-4Form.htm). Tests given for use in biomedical research that is conducted to generate scientific knowledge about genes, to learn about the genetic basis of disease, or for developing pharmaceutical and other treatment of disease are not included in the definition of a *genetic test* (Ariz. Rev. Stat. Ann. §12.2801). **Restriction on Disclosure by Insurers** Medical information may not be released by insurance companies; however, releases of information for research purposes without individual consent are permitted when the subject is not identified in research reports (Ariz. Rev. Stat. § 20-2113).
Florida	**Ownership and Restriction on Disclosure** The results of such DNA analysis, whether held by a public or private entity, are the exclusive property of the person tested, are confidential, and may not be disclosed without the consent of the person tested (Fla. Stat. Ann. 760.40(2)(a)).
Georgia	**Ownership and Restriction on Disclosure** Genetic information is the unique property of the individual tested (Ga. Code Ann. § 33-54-1). Genetic information may not be used or disclosed by any person without the owner's specific informed consent, subject to certain exceptions, such as use in anonymous research where the identity of any person tested is not disclosed to any third party (Ga. Code Ann. §§ 33-54-2 to -8).

consent for collection of genetic information from individuals should expressly clarify the rights of the parties to use and profit from discoveries based on such information. For research governed by the FDA, informed consent documents cannot contain exculpatory language that requires subjects to relinquish any of their legal rights.[56] Likewise, federal guidance for researchers governed by the Common Rule indicates that statements that the subject "donate," "give up all claim," or "give up property rights in tissue or data" are not acceptable for an informed consent document. It is acceptable, however, for such consent form to say that there are no plans to compensate the subject and the subject authorizes use of tissue samples or information for research purposes.[57]

Genetic information may be disclosed for anonymous research purposes in certain states, such as Georgia, without the specific consent of the subject of the information. The requirement that the data be anonymous is a more stringent standard than the HIPAA deidentification standard (i.e., data for which there is a very low risk that the individual who is the subject of the information could be reidentified based on the information alone or in combination with other reasonably available information). Anonymous data generally means that the individual *cannot* be identified based on the data. Therefore, it is likely insufficient to use the safe harbor method to deidentify PHI that is genetic information for research uses. A statistical standard for such deidentification would be required.

5.7 CONCLUSION

In light of the US regulatory scheme governing the privacy of individually identifiable health information, businesses that are considering collection and use of health data should map the flow of data and the type of data to develop appropriate, legally compliant strategies that would facilitate any potential or proposed secondary uses of such data. Strategies for including health information in Big Data must address authorization and consent for prospective uses of data received from covered entities or entities subject to state law. If data is collected directly from individuals, then the data collector's use and subsequent disclosure of such information will likely not be restricted by HIPAA or other federal regulations. However, such businesses may be subject to state law, either if a state law applies directly to businesses that maintain medical information or if a state law governs a person who obtains certain sensitive health information. Therefore, the proposed uses of sensitive information may be more limited, and the businesses' ability to redisclose such information will generally be restricted. If such Big Data includes genetic information, informed consent regarding the commercialization of the data and data ownership should be addressed.

NOTES

1. McKinsey Global Institute. Big Data: The Next Frontier for Innovation, Competition, and Productivity. McKinsey & Company, 2011. Available at http://www.mckinsey.com/insights/business_technology/big_data_the_next_frontier_for_innovation.
2. 42 U.S.C. §§ 1320d-1–1320-d- and its implementing regulations at 45 C.F.R. Parts 160 and 164.
3. 45 C.F.R. § 160.103. PHI is defined to include individually identifiable health information that (1) is created or received by covered entities, that is, health plans, health care clearinghouses, and certain health care providers that engage in standard electronic administrative and financial transactions regulated by HIPAA ("covered health care providers"), such as claims submission or health plan enrollment; and (2) relates to the past, present, or future physical or mental health or condition of an individual, the provision of health care to an individual, or the past, present, or future payment for the provision of health care to an individual (including demographic information); and (3) identifies the individual or with respect to which there is a reasonable basis to believe the information can be used to identify the individual.
4. 45 C.F.R. §160.103.
5. US Department of Health and Human Services (HHS). Personal Health Records and the HIPAA Privacy Rule. Available at http://www.hhs.gov/ocr/privacy/hipaa/understanding/special/healthit/phrs.pdf. Federal Trade Commission (FTC) regulations define a *personal health record* as an electronic record of "identifiable health information on an individual that can be drawn from multiple sources and that is managed, shared, and controlled by or primarily for the individual." 16 C.F.R. §318.2(d).
6. 42 U.S.C. §290dd and its implementing regulations at 42 C.F.R. Part 2.
7. 5 U.S.C. § 552a.
8. 42 U.S.C. § 263a, 42 C.F.R. Part 493.
9. 15 U.S.C. § 6801 et seq.
10. 29 U.S.C. § 1002 et seq.
11. 45 C.F.R. § 160.203.
12. 45 C.F.R. §160.103; PHI is any information about health status, provision of health care, or payment for health care that can be linked to a specific individual. This is interpreted rather broadly and includes any part of a patient's medical record or payment history.
13. 45 C.F.R. §164.502(b).
14. 45 C.F.R. § 160.103. Note that a covered entity may also serve as a business associate.
15. 45 C.F.R. § 164.506(c)(5).
16. 45 C.F.R. § 164.520(d).
17. *Health care operations* are certain administrative, financial, legal, and quality improvement activities of a covered entity that are necessary to run its business and to support the core functions of treatment and payment. These activities, which are limited to the activities listed in the definition of health care operations at 45 C.F.R. § 164.501, include conducting quality assessment and improvement activities, population-based activities relating to improving health or reducing health care costs, and case management and care coordination; reviewing the competence or qualifications of health care professionals, evaluating provider and health plan performance, training health care and non-health care professionals, accreditation,

certification, licensing, or credentialing activities; underwriting and other activities relating to the creation, renewal, or replacement of a contract of health insurance or health benefits and ceding, securing, or placing a contract for reinsurance of risk relating to health care claims; conducting or arranging for medical review, legal, and auditing services, including fraud and abuse detection and compliance programs; business planning and development, such as conducting cost management and planning analyses related to managing and operating the entity; and business management and general administrative activities, including those related to implementing and complying with the Privacy Rule and other Administrative Simplification Rules, customer service, resolution of internal grievances, sale or transfer of assets, creating deidentified health information or a limited dataset, and fundraising for the benefit of the covered entity.

18. Covered entities may disclose PHI for their own health care operations or may disclose PHI to another covered entity for certain health care operation activities of the entity that receives the information if (1) each entity either has or had a relationship with the individual who is the subject of the information and the PHI pertains to the relationship; and (2) the disclosure is for a quality-related health care operations activity or for the purpose of health care fraud and abuse detection or compliance; 45 C.F.R. §164.506(c).

19. HHS, Medicare Program. Medicare Shared Savings Program: Accountable Care Organizations; Final Rule, 76 Fed. Reg. 67802 (Nov. 2, 2011).

20. 45 C.F.R. § 164.514(a)–(c). It is important to know that the Privacy Rule permits a covered entity to assign to, and retain with, the deidentified health information, a code or other means of record reidentification if that code is not derived from or related to the information about the individual and is not otherwise capable of being translated to identify the individual. For example, an encrypted individual identifier (e.g., a Social Security number) would not meet the conditions for use as a reidentification code for deidentified health information because it is derived from individually identified information. In addition, the covered entity may not (1) use or disclose the code or other means of record identification for any purposes other than as a reidentification code for the deidentified data and (2) disclose its method of reidentifying the information.

21. 45 C.F.R. § 164.514(b)(2).

22. 45 C.F.R. § 164.514(b)(1); HHS, Office for Civil Rights (OCR). Guidance Regarding Methods for De-identification of Protected Health Information in Accordance with the Health Insurance Portability and Accountability Act (HIPAA) Privacy Rule. Available at http://www.gpo.gov/fdsys/pkg/FR-2011-11-02/pdf/2011-27461.pdf.

23. 45 C.F.R. § 164.504(e)(2)(ii)(A).

24. See 45 C.F.R. § 45, C.F.R. § 160.103 definition of business associate.

25. See OCR, Guidance Regarding Methods.

26. 45 C.F.R. § 164.502(a).

27. 45 C.F.R. § 164.502(a)(5)(ii); other permissible purposes are treatment and payment; a sale and merger transaction involving the covered entity or the business associate; activities performed by a business associate for or on behalf of the covered entity (or by a business associate subcontractor for or on behalf of the business associate) if the payment is for the business associate's performance of such activities (or for the subcontractor's performance of such activities); providing an access or an accounting to an individual; as required by law; and as otherwise permitted under HIPAA, where only a reasonable, cost-based fee is paid (or such other fee as permitted by law).

Although this last exclusion is not well defined, it involves situations for which authorization from the individual is received and patient information is aggregated and deidentified, as discussed previously.

28. 45 C.F.R. § 164.508(a)(4).
29. *Steinberg v. CVS Caremark Corp.*, 899 F. Supp. 2d 331, 338 (E.D. Pa. 2012).
30. Both the Common Rule and HIPAA define research as a "systematic investigation . . . designed to develop or contribute to generalizable knowledge." See 45 C.F.R. § 46.102(d) and 45 C.F.R. § 164.501.
31. 45 C.F.R. § 164.514(e).
32. 45 C.F.R. § 164.514(d).
33. 45 C.F.R. § 164.512(i).
34. 45 C.F.R. § 164.508.
35. HHS, OCR. Research. Available at http://www.hhs.gov/ocr/privacy/hipaa/understanding/coveredentities/research.html.
36. HHS. Modifications to the HIPAA Privacy, Security, Enforcement, and Breach Notification Rules Under the Health Information Technology for Economic and Clinical Health Act and the Genetic Information Nondiscrimination Act; Other Modifications to the HIPAA Rules, Final Rule, 78 Fed. Reg. 5566 (Jan. 25, 2013).
37. HHS, OCR. Research.
38. For studies that began prior to March 26, 2013, covered entities and researchers may permissibly rely on an IRB-approved consent that reasonably informed individuals of the future research, even though the HIPAA authorization relates (as was required) only to a specific study; see HHS, Modifications to the HIPAA.
39. 45 C.F.R. Part 46, Subpart A.
40. 21 C.F.R. Part 50.
41. The FDA regulations apply only to research over which the FDA has jurisdiction, primarily research involving investigational products; the Common Rule applies primarily to federally funded research or research at academic or other institutions that have an agreement to comply with the Common Rule.
42. National Institutes of Health, National Cancer Institute. Providing Your Tissue for Research. n.d. Available at http://www.cancer.gov/clinicaltrials/learningabout/providing-tissue.
43. Under the Privacy Rule, neither blood nor tissue, in and of itself, is considered individually identifiable health information; therefore, research involving only the collection of blood or tissue would not be subject to the Privacy Rule's requirements. However, to the extent that blood and tissue are labeled with information (e.g., admission date or medical record number), the Privacy Rule considers it individually identifiable and thus PHI. A covered entity's use or disclosure of this information for research is subject to the Privacy Rule. In addition, the results from an analysis of blood and tissue, if containing or associated with individually identifiable information, would be PHI. See HHS, National Institutes of Health. Research Repositories, Databases, and the HIPAA Privacy Rule. 2004. Available at http://privacyruleandresearch.nih.gov/research_repositories.asp. Note, however, that tissue banking may be subject to state tissue banking laws, the Anatomical Gift Act, and FDA regulations that establish specific requirements.
44. 45 C.F.R. § 164.508(a)(2).
45. HHS, OCR, Personal Health Records.

46. 16 C.F.R. Part 318; PHR-related entities include entities that interact with a vendor of PHRs either by offering products or services through the vendor's website or by accessing information or transmitting information to a PHR. Many businesses that offer web-based apps for health information fall into this category.

47. HHS, OCR. Frequently Asked Questions, How Do HIPAA Authorizations Apply to an Electronic Health Information Exchange Environment? December 15, 200-8. http://www.hhs.gov/ocr/privacy/hipaa/faq/health_information_technology/554.html; 45 C.F.R. § 164.508(c).2(a)(1)(i).

48. HHS, OCR, Personal Health Records.

49. FTC. FTC to Host Public Forum on Threats to Mobile Devices on June 4. February 22, 2013. Available at http://www.ftc.gov/news-events/press-releases/2013/02/ftc-host-public-forum-threats-mobile-devices-june-4.

50. How Target Figured Out a Teen Girl Was Pregnant Before Her Father Did. *Forbes*, February 16, 2012.

51. Lisa M. Boyle. *A Guide to Health Care Privacy*. Wolters Kluwer's Law and Business, last updated November 2013. Aspen Publishers Distribution Center, Frederick, MD.

52. Many states also have specific laws related to tissue banking and anatomical gifts, which require further consideration in creation of research repositories.

53. Cal. Civil Code § 56.06.

54. Cal. Civil Code § 56.05(f); "Individually identifiable: means that the medical information includes or contains any element of personal identifying information sufficient to allow identification of the individual (such as the patient's name, address, electronic mail address, telephone number, or Social Security number), or other information that reveals the individual's identity."

55. Cal. Civil Code § 56.11.

56. 21 C.F.R. § 50.20.

57. HHS, Office for Human Research Protections. Exculpatory Language in Informed Consent. November 15, 1996. Available at http://www.hhs.gov/ohrp/policy/exculp.html.

6

Big Data and Risk Assessment

Eileen R. Ridley

6.1 INTRODUCTION

The benefits of Big Data touch almost every aspect of digitized life: entertainment, academia, health, commercial enterprise, and governmental operations. However, with its breadth of reach comes greater exposure to risk and litigation. Significantly, the issue of privacy in the context of mass digitized information is relatively new. For a period of time, the public was enthralled with the benefits of the personal computer, the Internet, and personal mobile devices that made access to information available at literally a touch of a button. The conveniences provided by these technological advances distracted attention away from the realities of how those conveniences were provided, that is, via the collection, analysis, and distribution of data. However, as the public became more educated in how the new technological world worked, it became more concerned with how personal information was retained and distributed. Indeed, public awareness has been further heightened by various scandals, such as the recent revelations regarding the National Security Agency's (NSA's) use of digitized information, which in turn has spawned further privacy litigation. Big Data (as distinct from the issue of privacy alone) is a relatively recent evolution of the use of data. It is therefore likely that, with increased public awareness of Big Data and its uses, there will be new legal challenges and litigation focused on individual privacy rights and the principles of transparency, notice, access, and choice in the context of Big Data.

Although there are relatively few published cases discussing litigation of Big Data issues, those that do exist provide instruction for companies engaged in Big Data analytics. In short, companies must ensure transparency and simultaneously establish the business rationale for the use of Big Data. Moreover, when constructing mechanisms to use Big Data, companies should build in processes to retain and preserve their analytics in the case of litigation.

6.2 WHAT IS THE STRATEGIC PURPOSE FOR THE USE OF BIG DATA?

Although the commercial benefits of the use of Big Data are apparent, in the context of limiting risk, it is important for companies to be clear regarding the business purpose for the use of Big Data (and ensure their Big Data applications follow that purpose). This identification has proven to be particularly useful in the context of litigation. Indeed, courts frequently weigh the importance of the business purpose (and whether the use of Big Data exceeds that purpose) with the claimed violation of privacy (and whether the claimant was informed of the company's intended use of the data). For companies with business models dependent on the use of Big Data, risk is best mitigated by establishing the commercial and public value of their business model.

Most recently, this principle was proven in litigation between Google Inc., and the Authors Guild Inc.[1] The case concerned the Google Books Project; Google would scan books (including copyrighted books) and use optical character recognition technology to generate machine-readable text, thereby creating a digital copy of each book. Google then would analyze each scan and create an overall index of all the scanned books. The index, in turn, allows for a search for a particular word or phrase throughout the scanned works. Google included certain security measures to prevent users from viewing a complete copy of the works by permitting snippet views. In deciding in favor of Google against claims of copyright infringement by the authors, the court noted that there were many benefits of the project including (1) the creation of an efficient method of finding books; (2) the creation of a research tool; (3) improvement of interlibrary lending; and (4) the facilitation of finding and checking citations. Significantly, the court also noted (as a benefit) that the project promoted "data mining" or "text mining." Data mining or text mining is essentially the analysis of Big Data to produce results specific to a particular inquiry (e.g., is a particular word used, is a particular product in demand, etc.). The court considered data mining a research tool and noted that the project permitted researchers to track the frequency of references and how word uses had changed over time, thereby providing insights about "'fields as diverse as lexicography, the evolution of grammar, collective memory, the adoption of technology, the pursuit of fame, censorship, and historical epidemiology.'"[2] Indeed, in ruling for Google, the court went out of its way to note that the public benefit of the use of Big Data and data mining supported its ruling:

> In my view, Google Books provides significant public benefits. It advances the progress of the arts and sciences, while maintaining respectful consideration for the rights of authors and other creative individuals, and without adversely impacting the rights of copyright holders. It has become an invaluable research tool that permits students, teachers, librarians, and others to more efficiently identify and locate books. It has given scholars the ability, for the first time, to conduct full-text searches of tens of millions of books. It preserves books, in particular out-of-print and old books that have been forgotten in the bowels of libraries, and it gives them new life. It facilitates access to books for print-disabled and remote or underserved populations. It generates new audiences and creates new sources of income for authors and publishers. Indeed, all society benefits.[3]

Thus, Google successfully avoided liability by clearly defining the business purpose of its use of Big Data prior to the litigation, cogently presenting that vision to the court, and emphasizing to the court the public benefits of the results. Significantly, Google was successful in the face of the authors' claims to copyright, which typically trump mere claims of commercial interest in disputed works. However, the court found Google's competing commercial interests (e.g., attracting customers to purchase books) to be compelling. However, Google's use of Big Data analytics to create a public good (e.g., developing research tools) while providing some protection to the claimant's rights (notably Google prevented users from seeing a complete copyrighted work) enabled it to derive additional commercial benefit from its use of Big Data. The lesson: The litigation risk of using Big Data can be mitigated by a defined business purpose that (1) includes transparency so that the consumer is informed regarding how the data is being used; (2) provides protections for any competing commercial interests, and (3) promotes the advancement of the public good.

6.3 HOW DOES THE USE OF BIG DATA HAVE AN IMPACT ON THE MARKET?

Another issue that companies using Big Data should consider in the context of risk assessment is how the use of Big Data will have an impact on the marketplace. Generally, these questions go to whether there might be a claim that the use of the data would provide the basis for business claims like unfair competition. In reviewing these issues, companies should fully assess the market power Big Data analytics provide for the company, its vendors, and its competitors (see also Chapter 8, "The Antitrust Laws and Big Data"). This is particularly true when the company's use of Big Data analytics provides it with a commercial benefit at the expense of another company's commercial interest. Two recent cases highlight this issue.

In *PeopleBrowsr, Inc. v. Twitter, Inc.*, the court noted that viable state court claims could be raised as a result of Twitter's sudden exclusion of PeopleBrowsr from receipt of Twitter's "Big Data analytics" market.[4] Twitter's Big Data analytics market consisted of companies that used data-mining techniques to derive insights from the flow of information generated on Twitter. In other words, Twitter provided companies with raw data that assisted those companies in marketing their products and services. Thus, a soft drink maker could gather information to determine if its new product was trending on Twitter, which in turn could be used as a measure of the effectiveness of its marketing campaign. PeopleBrowsr participated in the market for over four years, receiving every tweet posted on Twitter through the Twitter "Firehose" and paid Twitter over $1 million per year for such access. As the court noted: "PeopleBrowsr analyzes tweets to sell information to its clients, such as insight regarding consumer reactions to products and services as well as identification of the Twitter users who have the most influence in certain locations and communities."[5] After having such access, Twitter decided to identify favored companies to exert more control over the Twitter Big Data analytics market. PeopleBrowsr was not one of those favored and brought an action for, among other claims, unfair competition. PeopleBrowsr not only obtained a preliminary injunction against Twitter but also successfully defended against Twitter's attempt to move the case to federal court and dismiss the action.

Apparently, the court in *PeopleBrowsr* found Twitter's actions to be arbitrary and potentially predatory (by unilaterally trying to control and narrow its self-created Big Data analytics market). The lesson: In the age of Big Data, companies not only must be sensitive to how they deal with consumer information but also must consider the market effects of providing their Big Data analytics to third parties—including how they determine which parties will receive such information. As brokers of Big Data analytics, companies face significant litigation risk if their actions to create, narrow, or redefine their market are considered capricious. Again, transparency and a defined business model expressly addressing the use of Big Data are critical to limit a company's risk.

Another instructive case is *Tiffany (NJ), Inc. v. eBay, Inc.*[6] In this case, Tiffany had identified that items had been sold on eBay Inc. that were not genuine Tiffany products. Tiffany, of course, is a famous jeweler, and eBay is an online marketplace. Tiffany sought to protect its trademarks in a suit against eBay, contending that eBay was obligated to prohibit sellers from placing counterfeit Tiffany items on the market. How does this relate to Big Data? Tiffany presented the somewhat novel argument that eBay, as a vast online marketplace, had access to an enormous amount of data and had instituted fraud protocols that enabled it to analyze the data to assist in identifying suspect vendors. In essence, Tiffany contended that eBay was *obligated* to use its Big Data capabilities to root out forgeries and police the marketplace. Indeed, an expert for Tiffany testified that

> using data mining techniques commonly used by corporations, eBay could have designed programs that identified listings of Tiffany items likely to be counterfeit, and that identified sellers thereof, using an algorithm to produce a "suspiciousness" score.[7]

Ultimately, the court rejected this contention, noting, for purposes of trademark claims, the rights holder (i.e., Tiffany) was obligated to show that eBay actually knew that specific items that purported to be Tiffany products were in fact forgeries. Tiffany could not meet this standard. Further, the court noted that the law did not obligate eBay to use its Big Data capability to police the site. However, the court took pains to note the following:

> The result of the application of this legal standard is that Tiffany must ultimately bear the burden of protecting its trademark. Policymakers may yet decide that the law as it stands is inadequate to protect rights of owners in light of the increasing scope of Internet commerce and the concomitant rise in potential trademark infringement. Nevertheless, under the law as

it currently stands, it does not matter whether eBay or Tiffany could more efficiently bear the burden of policing the eBay website for Tiffany counterfeits—an open question left unresolved by this trial.[8]

Thus, the court seems to warn that companies with the capacity to employ Big Data analytics may be compelled to do so to protect fair competition and their commercial marks (indeed, the court noted that Tiffany could have used the same data-mining techniques it suggested eBay employ to protect Tiffany's trademark).[9] In other words, although a company may develop its Big Data capabilities for its own commercial benefit, those same capabilities may require it to proactively protect not only their own separate commercial interests (such as copyrights, trademarks, and patents) but also those of others. This is particularly true when the business model entails the use of another company's product (and the associated trade rights), such as eBay. It is unlikely that any court would require a company to incur extraordinary expense to protect another's commercial interest. However, if doing so would subject a company to relatively nominal cost, courts will be more likely to assign that obligation on the entity. Thus, companies that employ Big Data analytics should not only consider how those analytics might increase their market share but also consider how the same analytic capability might be employed to deter claims by the public, competitors, and vendors. For example, data analytics can be used to police websites to identify possible breaches and forgeries while also providing the basis to thwart competitive challenges (e.g., if the data analytics not only provides a competitive advantage but also fosters general public knowledge). Further, data analytics may also be employed to assist companies in responding to discovery should litigation ensue.

6.4 DOES THE USE OF BIG DATA RESULT IN INJURY OR DAMAGE?

For any litigation claim to stand, the plaintiff must establish that the attributed conduct by the company resulted in injury or damage. In the privacy and Big Data context, however, proving injury or damage can frequently be a high hurdle to jump.

Two decisions offer a case study. The first, *In re JetBlue Airways Corp. Privacy Litig.*, concerned the creation of passenger name records (PNRs) by airlines and their use by other entities.[10] JetBlue (like other airlines) had a practice of compiling and maintaining personal information (the PNRs) of passengers. The PNRs typically included the passenger names, addresses, phone numbers, and travel itineraries and were obtained through flight bookings either telephonically or online. Acxiom provides customer and information management solutions and separately maintained personally identifiable information on almost 80% of the US population. After September 11, 2001, a data-mining company (DMC), Torch, approached the Department of Defense (DoD) and suggested it could help enhance security by analyzing information contained in the PNRs to identify persons seeking access to military installations and predicting which individuals might pose a security risk. The DoD agreed to the plan and allowed airline PNRs to be a data source for the project. JetBlue was contacted by Torch, through the DoD, to provide its PNR data, which it did (without compensation). Torch combined this information with data from Acxiom, which constituted approximately five million electronically stored PNRs. Merging the data resulted in Torch obtaining a single database of JetBlue passenger information, including each passenger's name, address, gender, home ownership or rental status, economic status, Social Security number, occupation, and the number of adults and children in the passenger's family as well as the number of vehicles owned or leased. Torch used this data to create a profiling scheme regarding high-risk passengers.[11] JetBlue acknowledged that providing the PNRs was a violation of the company's privacy policy (e.g., no consent by JetBlue's customers was obtained for the transfer of the information). A class of plaintiffs then brought the litigation claiming violations of various privacy statutes (including the Electronic Communications Privacy Act, ECPA) and state common law claims. The court determined that there was no liability under the ECPA because the statute is only applicable to "electronic communication services," which involve a "service which provides to users the ability to send or receive wire or electronic communications" (18 U.S.C. Section 2510(15)). JetBlue is not such a service and therefore was not liable under the ECPA. More important for this discussion, the court further ruled that JetBlue was not liable for the remaining claims because the plaintiffs could not establish damage or injury. Specifically, the court noted that "[i]t is apparent based on the briefing and oral argument held in this case that the sparseness of the damages allegations is a direct result of plaintiffs' inability to plead or prove any actual contract [or other] damages. As plaintiffs' counsel concedes, the only damage that can be read into the present complaint is a loss of privacy."[12] However, a loss of privacy alone (e.g., without an economic loss) does not constitute injury or damage that would support a claim.

In contrast, there is the decision in *Fraley v. Facebook, Inc.*[13] *Fraley* concerned Facebook's "Sponsored Stories" application of Big Data. Facebook is a social networking site that, as of 2011, had over 600 million members. Facebook generates its revenue through the sale of advertising targeted at its users. Sponsored Stories was an advertising practice whereby if a Facebook member "liked" an advertiser's Facebook page or advertisement, the advertiser's information and ad would appear on the member's friends' pages indicating that the member liked the advertiser. Essentially, it appeared that the member "sponsored" the advertiser's ad on the member's friends' pages (thus, suggesting that the member was recommending to his or her Facebook friends to solicit the advertiser). The court found that the plaintiff's claims against Facebook were viable and, distinguishing *JetBlue*, found sufficient claims for damage or injury. Specifically, the *Fraley* court stated that:

> Here, by contrast, Plaintiffs have articulated a coherent theory of how they were economically injured by the misappropriation of their names, photographs, and likenesses for use in paid commercial endorsements targeted not at themselves, but at *other* consumers, without their consent. Unlike the plaintiffs in [other cases], Plaintiffs here do not allege that their personal browsing histories have economic value to advertisers wishing to target advertisements at Plaintiffs themselves, nor that their demographic information has economic value for general marketing and analytics purposes. Rather they allege that their individual, personalized endorsement of products, services, and brands to their friends and acquaintances has concrete, provable value in the economy at large, which can be measured by additional profit Facebook earns from selling Sponsored Stories compared to its sale of regular advertisements. . . . Furthermore, Plaintiffs do not merely cite abstract economic concepts in support of their theory of economic injury, but rather point to specific examples of how their personal endorsement is valued by advertisers. The [Second Amended Complaint] quotes Facebook CEO Mark Zuckerberg stating that "[a] trusted referral influences people more that the best broadcast message. A trusted referral is the Holy Grail of advertising."[14]

Thus, by recognizing the economic value of member-sponsored advertisements but failing to obtain members' consent, Facebook's use of Big Data analytics created a damage model for plaintiffs.

The immediate lesson of these two cases is that a plaintiff must be able to show a damage or injury to successfully present privacy claims. However, there is also a greater lesson. In both *JetBlue* and *Facebook*, there was a failure of transparency. Information was gathered and used for purposes that the consumers neither had knowledge of nor permitted. In *JetBlue*, the gathering and transfer of the information was admittedly *against the stated privacy policy of the company.* Such violations of stated policies combined with the failure to inform consumers regarding the use of their information is a sure recipe for litigation. Indeed, as the public becomes more educated concerning the amount of information gathered and its uses, it has been more likely to bring lawsuits to limit the use of that information. Moreover, when information is provided to a commercial entity that is then transferred (without notice or permission) to a governmental interest, public concern and the risk of litigation are heightened. This is best and most recently illustrated by the NSA scandal regarding the monitoring of the public's use of the Internet. It is a cautionary tale to companies who have harnessed the power of Big Data: Be clear regarding what information is obtained, how it will be used, and whether (and in what circumstances) it will be transferred. Failure to do so will result in increased exposure to litigation.

6.5 DOES THE USE OF BIG DATA ANALYSIS HAVE AN IMPACT ON HEALTH ISSUES?

As discussed in Chapter 4, "Privacy and Big Data," the benefits and dangers of using Big Data analytics may be most dramatic in the health field. This is not only because of the very personal and sensitive nature of the data but also because of the vast amounts of data involved as almost all people have entered the health marketplace in some way. The key to limiting risk exposure in the health context, as noted previously in this chapter, is deidentification.

London v. New Albertson's, Inc. is a good example of this concept.[15] The *London* case was primarily based on claimed violations of California's Medical Information Act (CMIA), California Civil Code Section 56 et seq. Factually, the suit concerned the alleged sale of pharmacy customer prescription information to DMCs, which used that information for marketing purposes. New Albertson's owned several stores that contained pharmacies.

London had his prescriptions filled at one of those stores. According to the allegations of the suit, the DMCs installed software on the pharmacies' mainframe computer servers that captures and collates patient prescription information as it is transferred to the DMCs' offsite computer servers. The software deidentifies the prescription information and assigns a number to each patient to allow correlation of that information without individually identifying patients. Once the DMCs harvest the deidentified data, they combine it with proscriber reference information and sell this information to pharmaceutical companies, which in turn use it to structure drug-marketing programs directed to physicians.[16] The court found that the plaintiff had not made a viable claim of violation of the California Medical Information Act (CMIA) because the information was deidentified; therefore, there was no transmission of "medical information" as defined by the CMIA because the information could not be traced back to the individual once deidentified. While the Court's holding in *London* speaks to the risk-limiting value of deidentification of health information, it is important to note that London was allowed to amend his claims to assert a more viable claim. Further, it is important to note that the deidentification took place *after the information was transferred by New Albertson's to the DMCs*, thus there might be a viable claim for the transfer to the DMCs given the lack of consent for the use of the information by London.

Another instructional case regarding the use of health data is *IMS Health, Inc. v. Sorrell*.[17] There, the appellant challenged a Vermont statute banning the sale, transmission, or use of prescriber-identifiable data (PI data) for marketing or promoting a prescription drug without prescriber consent. The appellate court found the statute was unconstitutional as a commercial speech restriction. In so doing, the court noted that the data was deidentified; therefore, there was no great harm that raised the state's interest in the statute's application. Notwithstanding the court's ruling, there were important points raised by the dissent, including the issue of when the information was deidentified:

> Accordingly, before a detailer ever sets foot in a doctor's office—that is, before the commercial speech the majority focuses on ever occurs—at least three events take place: first, a pharmacy gathers information from patients seeking to fill prescriptions; second, it collects and sells that data to third parties, principally, "data vendors" or "data miners" such as appellants here; and third, these data miners repackage that data and license it to pharmaceutical companies.[18]

Thus, the dissent noted there could be significant litigation risks in providing health-related Big Data to third parties prior to deidentification—whether or not the information was later deidentified for commercial purposes. There are two lessons here. First, given the sensitive nature of personal health information, there are great risks of failing to comply with privacy standards. Second, the key to reduce risk exposure is not only the use of deidentification but also when that process is employed. If the personal health information is transferred improperly, subsequent deidentification will not serve to protect a company from the risk of litigation.

6.6 THE IMPACT OF BIG DATA ON DISCOVERY

Putting aside potential liability exposure that might arise from the use of Big Data analytics, companies should also consider the impact of Big Data on discovery. This impact is twofold. First, Big Data has an impact on the amount of information that might be subject to discovery in litigation—especially if Big Data analytics play a part in company business strategy. Second, Big Data can be used in the context of discovery to assist in searching for relevant evidence. These points are discussed in detail in Chapter 11, "Big Data Discovery," but are touched on in this section.

The first point was discussed at length in *Chevron Corp. v. Weinberg Group*.[19] In *Chevron*, the court was dealing with a discovery motion related to the review of privilege in a wide-ranging environmental matter. The court noted that "... in the era of 'b'ig 'd'ata, in which storage capacity is cheap and several bankers' boxes of documents can be stored with a keystroke on a three inch thumb drive, there are simply more documents that everyone is keeping and a concomitant necessity to log more of them."[20] The judge further noted its own limited capacity to review the volume of information produced by Big Data discovery:

> In an earlier time, the insufficiency of the log defaulted to in camera review by the judge. Yet, in case such as this, the sheer number of documents on a log may make that impossible. Here, I would have to review 9,171 pages of documents. That seems inconceivable given my advanced years. In all seriousness, a judge, unlike lawyers, who have resources for culling through documents, cannot use technology-assisted review to do the review more efficiently.

The discussion in *Chevron* highlights the two issues regarding Big Data analytics in discovery. First, in the era of Big Data, discovery will necessarily cover huge amounts of data, which in turn can be very expensive. Indeed, court decisions indicate that the cost of e-vendors to review such data is not a recoverable cost.[21] Thus, the expense of data review is borne by the company itself—even if it successfully defends against the litigation. Second, if a company has adopted the use of Big Data analytics, it should design its systems and programs to provide for the possibility of litigation. This means designing methods to determine what analytics are used and preserve the results of the programs—particularly if those analytics support strategic business plans.

NOTES

1. *Authors Guild, Inc. v. Google, Inc.*, 2013 U.S. Dist. LEXIS 162198 (So. Dist. of NY, November 14, 2013).
2. *Id.*, 2013 U.S. Dist. LEXIS 162198, at *9–11.
3. *Id.*, 2013 U.S. Dist. LEXIS 162198, at *27–28.
4. *PeopleBrowsr, Inc. v. Twitter, Inc.*, 2013 U.S. Dist. LEXIS 31786; 2013 WL 843032 (U.S. Dist. Ct., Northern District of CA, March 6, 2013).
5. *Id.*, 2013 U.S. Dist. LEXIS, 31786, at *2–3.
6. *Tiffany (NJ), Inc. v. eBay, Inc.*, 576 F.Supp.2d 463 (U.S. Dist. Ct., So. Dist. of NY, July 14, 2008).
7. *Id.*, at 576 F. Supp.2d, 463, 491–492.
8. *Id.* 576 F.Supp.2d 463, at *470.
9. *Id.*, 576 F.Supp.2d 463, at *492.
10. *In re JetBlue Airways Corp. Privacy Litig.*, 379 F.Supp.2d 299 (U.S. Dist. Ct., Eastern Dist. of NY, August 1, 2005).
11. *Id.*, 379 F.Supp.2d 299, at *304–305.
12. *Id.*, 379 F.Supp.2d 299, at *326.
13. *Fraley v. Facebook, Inc.*, 830 F.Supp.2d 785 (U.S. Dist. Ct. Northern Dist. of CA, December 16, 2011).
14. *Id.*, 830 F.Supp.2d 785, at 798–800.
15. *London v. New Albertson's, Inc.*, 2008 U.S. Dist. LEXUS 76246; 2008 WL 4492642 (U.S. Dist. Ct., So. Dist. of California, September 30, 2008).
16. *Id.*, 2008 U.S. Dist. LEXIS 76246, at *2–3.
17. *IMS Health, Inc. v. Sorrell*, 630 F.3d 263 (Ct. of Appeals, 2nd Cir., November 23, 2010).
18. *Id.*, 630 F.3d 263, at 283.
19. Chevron Corp. v. Weinberg Group, 286 F.R.D. 95 (U.S. Dist. Ct. D.C., September 26, 2012).
20. Id., 286 F.R.D. 95, at 98 – 99.
21. See, e.g., Race Tires AM., Inc., v. Hoosier Racing Tire Corp., 674 F. 3d158 (U.S. Ct. of Appeals, Third Circuit, March 16, 2012.

7

Licensing Big Data

Aaron K. Tantleff

7.1 OVERVIEW

This chapter discusses the licensing of databases. A license is nothing more than a contract between a licensor and licensee that defines the scope of activities a licensee may engage in with regard to the licensed database (e.g., use the data solely for internal use, distribute limited segments to others, combine the database with other data, etc.). Licenses are also used to ensure proper monetization of the data being licensed. Licenses in which a company will grant a third party the use of their database are referred to as "outbound" licenses. Licenses in which a business will be on the receiving end of a database license granted by a third party are called "inbound" licenses. Both types of licenses are discussed in this chapter.

One of the greatest mistakes in license agreements involving Big Data is the attempt to use a traditional license agreement (e.g., a form agreement used for licensing software or other forms of content) to govern a license of Big Data. As discussed in this material, a traditional license agreement is generally not appropriate and may result in a lack of adequate protection for the database, exposure for both the licensee and licensor, and a failure to realize appropriate revenue from exploitation of the data.

Under traditional database licensing agreements, the licensor was either the owner or, itself, a licensee (with the right to sublicense to others) of a database. The licensor would enter into an agreement with a licensee granting access to the database. Traditionally, the database was a structured set of data, made available either on a subscription basis or as a data feed. Under the traditional model, the license granted to the database was generally limited in scope; for example, to a defined set of data or for certain purposes. The licensee generally had a clear understanding of the data being made available to them and what they could do with it. However, it is not as straightforward with respect to Big Data. The data may consist of data that was generated by the licensor itself, from users and other third parties from which the licensor collects information, data licensed from third parties, and data that was scraped from the Internet, including via various social media tools. Accordingly, the licensor likely does not own or have an explicit license to all of the data it may offer to a licensee, and it is highly likely that a licensor may not be able to obtain one. Despite the absence of ownership or an explicit license to the data it is offering to license, a licensor may still have intellectual property rights in the data, which may permit the licensor the right to grant a license.

When drafting or negotiating a Big Data license agreement, licensors and licensees alike should consider certain key issues:

- Contractual and other legal protections for databases;
- Ownership of the data;
- Ensuring the scope of the license balances the licensor's desire to limit the scope of the rights granted as compared with a licensee's desire for expansive rights designed for a maximum opportunity to exploit and mine the database;
- Anonymization of the data;
- Confidentiality, both as a protection of Big Data and of licensee's information;
- "Salting" of the database or the use of fake data to uncover unauthorized use and copying of database;
- Each party's rights of termination;
- Limitations of liability governing each party's responsibility for damages;
- Fees to be charged and protection of the licensee from "fee creep";
- Audit rights to ensure proper use of the database;
- Warranties; and
- Indemnification obligations.

In the remainder of this chapter, each of these issues is discussed from the perspective of both the licensee and the licensor.

7.2 PROTECTION OF THE DATA/DATABASE UNDER INTELLECTUAL PROPERTY LAW

Over the years, there have been several unsuccessful attempts to create a new intellectual property right expressly designed to protect databases. In the absence of that clear right, database licensors have had to rely on a somewhat imperfect combination of copyright and trade secret law to protect their data. We say "imperfect" because neither law provides complete protection (e.g., copyright only protects the compilation of the database as a whole and trade secret law only protects databases that are not generally known and are the subject of efforts to protect their confidentiality). That said, the protections afforded under copyright and trade secret law should not be minimized. Each affords the licensor the ability to recover potentially substantial damages for misuse of its database. In some instances, the licensor may also be able to recover statutory damages (i.e., damages specified by law, without having to actually establish the amount of damages actually incurred by the licensor) and its attorney's fees and costs. Recovery is even permitted when the misuse was "innocent" (i.e., no malicious or wrongful intent need be shown to recover potential damages in some cases).

7.2.1 Copyright

Copyright protection affords the creator (referred to as the "author") of an original work with significant protections, such as the ability to control who has access to the copyrighted materials and how the copyrighted materials may be accessed, used, and modified. Copyright protection also provides the creator with the ability to take legal action against a party who improperly accessed, used, or disclosed the copyrighted material. The individual elements of data that make up a database are *not* generally copyrightable, but their compilation into a database is copyrightable.

A famous example illustrates the approach to copyright protection for databases. Consider someone's name, address, and telephone number. This information, standing alone, is not copyrightable. It is fact, not a "work of authorship" protected under copyright law. Now, consider the assembly of thousands, perhaps tens of thousands, of those names, addresses, and telephone numbers into an ordered database (i.e., a phone book). While copyright will not protect the individual entries in that phone book, it will protect the resulting compilation/database in the form of the phone book.

The same approach has been applied to afford many other types of databases copyright protection.

7.2.2 Trade Secrets

In some circumstances, the contents of a database may represent the trade secrets of a licensor. Trade secrets are governed by state law, and all states (excluding New York and Massachusetts), the District of Columbia, Puerto Rico, and the US Virgin Islands have adopted a variation of the Uniform Trade Secrets Act. A trade secret is a set of information or a compilation of information that is not generally known or reasonably ascertainable by others, by which a business can obtain an economic advantage over competitors or customers, and is the subject of reasonable efforts by its owner to maintain its confidentiality.

To ensure their databases have potential protection as a trade secret, licensors must include contractual protections to ensure the database is held in confidence and not disclosed to unauthorized parties. Licensees must be careful when accessing databases where the licensor is claiming trade secret protection. In many cases, the licensor may require the licensee to abide by certain safeguards that the licensee may not have the ability to comply with absent significant costs. However, in some instances, a licensee's standard information security practices are no less protective than the licensor's requirements. As a result, licensees need to thoroughly review the licensor's information security requirements and what they require. In an effort to ensure all "reasonable" efforts are employed to protect their information and to avoid having to review a licensee's information security standards, licensors often include generic language in their database license agreement with a reference holding the licensee accountable to the requirements as set forth in the licensor's standard information security guidelines. If a licensee does not carefully review these additional terms, it is possible that a licensee could be in breach of the license agreement the moment they accept it. Licensees should also look out for licensors who attempt to provide information security requirements that are inconsistent with the nature of the data licensed.

7.2.3 Contractual Protections for Big Data

As a complement to the intellectual property protections discussed, contractual limitations should be included to further protect databases from unauthorized use and disclosure. Most important, those limitations should include a clearly drafted license grant defining the rights of the licensee, a clause defining the licensor's ownership rights, and a properly worded confidentiality clause. Each party—licensor and licensee—will want to ensure these protections adequately represent their needs and expectations in the proposed license agreement. These and other contractual protections are discussed in the following sections.

7.3 OWNERSHIP RIGHTS

One of the key provisions in any license agreement is the language defining the parties' respective ownership rights with regard to the database. Data has intrinsic value. Owning the data imparts the ability for a party to control the right of a third party to access, create, modify, use, repurpose, make available to others, and sell data, as well as the ability to transfer and assign these rights to others. Accordingly, licensors and licensees regularly debate this issue. The licensor's desire is to control all access to and use of the database, as well as all modifications, enhancements, and other revisions (sometimes called "derivative works") of the database. This must be counterbalanced by the licensee's desire to fully exploit the database for its own purpose, which may be internal or external. For example, a licensee may license a database and then spend hundreds of hours mining the database for information generating analysis and new sets of data based on the derivative works of such data mining and analysis. The question will arise regarding whether the licensee or the licensor will claim ownership of derivative works such as this.

The owner of the data is generally the party that creates, generates, and collects the data. With respect to the traditional structured database, determining ownership is generally a straightforward process. However, with the rise of Big Data, resolving questions of ownership become more difficult, particularly because of the manner in which data is collected and generated. Big Data is the compilation of massive amounts of data collected from a variety of places using varying methods of collection. Ownership of Big Data is further complicated by the fact that, as data is collected, stored, and analyzed, new data is created based on the combination of the different elements from the database. In many cases, this new data is as valuable as, if not more valuable than, the data on which it is based.

There are two main principles of ownership fought over between licensors and licensees. Failure to address either of these up front may result in disastrous outcomes for all parties. The two most significant issues of ownership is who is the owner of the underlying, licensed data, and who is the owner of the derivative works produced as a result of the licensee's analysis of the licensed data.

With respect to the underlying data, a licensor should state, and the licensee should confirm, that as between the licensee and licensor, the licensor is the owner of the database, its content, and any algorithms contained therein. If this is not addressed up front, some licensees may challenge the licensor's ownership rights in and to the data or attempt to copy the data, claiming the licensor does not have any legal right to prevent a third party from copying the database and/or the database deserves no legal protection.

On the other hand, many license agreements are silent on the last concern; ownership of new data and other derivative works created from the exploitation of the licensed data. Failure to address this may interfere with or prevent the licensor from being able to license the database to other parties or frustrate a licensee that invested tremendous resources to mine and analyze the data. Given all the complications of Big Data, it is of tantamount importance to a licensor that it ensures that there are no encumbrances on its ability to license and derive profit from its database. Depending on the nature of the data and the particular analysis performed, general principles of common law provide that, absent a contractual agreement to the contrary, and despite the ownership of the underlying data, ownership of the derived data may default to licensee. It is also possible that ownership of the derivative works may be jointly owned by the licensee and licensor because the licensee performed analytics on data owned by licensor. While in many instances licensors are willing to grant ownership of such derived works to the licensee, some may request that such ownership is limited to the actual derivative works created between the parties as the licensor be unable to control or account for the analytics performed by other licensees or by other third parties. In other words, some licensors are concerned that two or more licensees may seek to perform the same or similar sets of analytics and that as a licensor it does not control licensee's authorized use of the data and cannot guarantee that other licensees are not performing the same or substantially similar types of analytics or that more than one licensee may have created similar derivative works.

If the licensor retains all rights in the derivative works, the licensee needs to take extra caution when combining the licensed data with that of its own. Where a licensor retains ownership in the derivate works, by combining a licensee's data with that of the licensor, then arguably a licensee may, unintentionally, assign ownership in licensee's own data to the licensor. If the licensor is granted a license to all derivate works, then the licensee may have inadvertently granted a license to the licensor in order to access and use the licensee's data. Either scenario could possibly result in a potential loss of the licensee's intellectual property, exposure of the licensee's data if not properly protected by the licensor's obligations of confidentiality, or a breach of third-party rights because of the use of the data beyond the consent or authorized use of such data.

On the other hand, licensees need to consider the efforts required to mine the database and whether the licensor's ownership rights, and thus control rights, would interfere with the licensee's ability to exploit the data. Licensees also have concerns as to their ability to restrict access to the data they generate. For example, what is to stop a licensor from selling a licensee's results to the licensee's competitors? Where a licensor demands ownership of a licensee's generated data, a licensee must ensure that it has a fully paid, royalty-free license without restriction on the use of the results.

Some licensees try to avoid this discussion by taking a different approach. When licensing Big Data, the volume and variety are so massive that some believe that it is highly unlikely that two unrelated entities would license or access the identical set of data or perform the same set of analytics over the identical dataset. Therefore, some licensees avoid the ownership debate by restricting a licensor's ability to provide the identical dataset to two different competitor companies. Such a provision may provide comfort to each of the parties as a licensee does not have to worry that its investment in licensing and mining the data will be wasted, and a licensor has little risk as the nature of Big Data databases change so rapidly that there is little chance of this occurring. Whether a licensee or licensor, this provision is highly dependent on the makeup of the database and how a licensor grants access to its database.

7.4 LICENSE GRANT

The license grant is one of the most significant provisions in the license agreement. It sets the tone for the entire engagement and defines the scope of the license, the restrictions placed on the licensee, the extent of the licensee's authorized use, and any other licensee obligations. This is often where the licensee and licensor first start to discuss the intentions that each party has with respect to the data. This analysis should also include a discussion of the rights and use of any results, analytics, or algorithms created by or to be used with the database.

In developing the license grant, it is important for both parties to think critically regarding all aspects of what is required to enable and protect both the licensee and licensor. One of the first questions any licensee should ask in contemplating a proposed license grant is whether this license grant will afford the licensee the ability to do everything currently contemplated with the data and whether and how to address predictable future uses.

Licensors should understand how they intend to license the applicable database. Generally, a licensor will only grant a nonexclusive license (i.e., the licensor is not precluded from licensing the same database to others, including potential competitors of the licensee, for the exact same purposes) for use of their database. A licensor generally intends to capitalize on its Big Data investment by licensing access to the database to as many licensees as possible. In addition, not only does a licensor want to reserve the right to offer the same license to other potential licensees, some licensors want to ensure their own right to mine the data. In addition to granting access to the database, some licensors may package and sell their own reports based on analytics performed by the licensor. Notwithstanding all this, some subsets of Big Data have the potential to provide a significant competitive advantage to a licensee, but only if such data is not provided to a licensee's competitors. If it is, such data may have little or no economic value to a licensee. In such instances, the licensee should request an exclusive license or a sole license, allowing the licensor to utilize and analyze the data solely for its own internal purposes.

Licensors, as discussed further in the section on fees, may wish to consider a licensee's ability to grant sublicenses to third parties to use the database, its ability to distribute the data, as well as any results from the licensee's analysis of the database. Generally, licensors are hesitant to grant a licensee the right to offer sublicenses as such sublicensee would not be under contract directly with the licensor. Granting sublicenses may also affect the licensor's ability to fully exploit the revenue potential derived from granting licenses to the database. However, in some cases, a licensee may not be the party best suited to analyze the data and therefore seeks to grant a sublicense to a third party to assist the licensee with the analysis. Failure to allow a licensee to grant such access may diminish the value of the license to a potential licensee. To address this concern, a licensor could establish reasonable limitations granting the applicable sublicense while restricting the sublicensee's performance to the benefit and on behalf of the licensee.

Licensors may also wish to carefully consider whether to allow licensees the ability to combine the licensed database with the licensee's database or any other unauthorized or preapproved data. There are a number of potential concerns, including for reasons affecting ownership, intellectual property rights, consent, and privacy. If the licensor is not careful in restricting what types of data are combined, the licensee could expose the licensor to significant liability arising from the combination of the licensor's data with other data. For example, the combination or aggregation of data may exceed the authorized scope of the licensor's data.

Data that has been collected and provided via a specific database may have been collected under a specific set of facts and circumstances, each with specific consents. These consents may limit the use of the data in a specific manner. When combining sets of disparate data, resulting in the aggregation of data into larger datasets, it becomes increasingly difficult to determine whether the use of such data is within the scope of the applicable original consent the data was collected under. It is also possible that by combining data with other databases one could engage in secondary activities or analyses that were not possible with the smaller dataset. With these new, secondary activities, new uses of the data become available, and one needs to consider whether these new uses were anticipated and consented to at the time the data was collected. If not, it might be possible that by aggregating the data, any such secondary use of the data would be out of the scope for which the consent was granted. It is also important from both the licensee's and licensor's perspective that, although the licensee's use of data or performance of certain analytics was allowable as originally licensed, the new, aggregated dataset may result in infringing activity. In such case, the licensee and licensor may be subject to potential third-party claims of infringement. For example, given that algorithms are protectable via patent as a business method claim, it is possible that the use of a certain algorithm on an aggregated set of data that was not previously cleared could result in a claim of patent infringement of such third party's business method patent.

As with every license agreement, regardless of how tightly drafted, there will always be something that was unanticipated or forgotten, or new abilities and rights with respect to the data will emerge that could not be anticipated. Therefore, all well-drafted license grants should end with the statement that "all rights not expressly granted in this provision are expressly reserved by licensor," ensuring that the licensor does not unintentionally give up its rights.

Given all the potential issues and liabilities, it is critical that the license grant does not exceed the scope of permitted use for the data. Any license grant provision should be clear and expressly state that the license to the data is limited to the authorized use as set forth in the agreement or in such other document attached to and made part of the license agreement. However, the need remains to be balanced against the broad and ever-increasing opportunities for use of Big Data and a licensee's desire to fully exploit the licensed data as intended by the license, subject to any legal limitations. Accordingly, a licensee should ensure that the license grant is sufficiently broad to allow the licensee to exploit the database for its intended manner.

7.5 ANONYMIZATION

Both licensors and licensees face significant potential liability and public relations challenges when working with Big Data sets given the risk of reidentifying individuals. Big Data has become so large that no matter what one does to deidentify individuals, Big Data enables anyone with the appropriate tools to potentially reidentify any deidentified individual.

Various regulations address the issue of anonymization and deidentification of data. The Health Insurance Portability and Accountability Act (HIPAA) of 1996 addresses the issue of deidentified data by providing for an expert determination and a safe harbor if certain key pieces of information are removed from the medical record.[1] The Gramm-Leach-Bliley Act also addresses the issue of anonymized data by defining *personally identifiable financial information* as that which "does not include information or blind data that does not contain personal identifiers such as account numbers, names or addresses."[2]

Notwithstanding the regulatory limitations on the use of personal information and the restrictions on reidentifying and targeting individuals, there is a real risk and a precedent of people being able to take datasets that claim to be anonymized and deidentified and identifying individuals. Even with the stringent requirements promulgated by HIPAA that are designed to ensure that a deidentified health care record would not be identifiable, using just publicly available data, one could reidentify patients who were previously thought to be anonymous.

Depending on the circumstances, licensors should consider including the following provisions designed to minimize the licensor's risk that an individual will be reidentified or targeted:

- Limiting the licensee's use of the database to datasets that have been anonymized;
- Prohibiting a licensee from reidentifying any individuals or combining the dataset with other datasets that would enable any individuals to be reidentified;
- Prohibiting licensees from using the data to take any action based on reidentified data;
- Prohibiting licensees from using the datasets for unauthorized purposes; and
- Requiring that the licensee notify the licensor in the event the licensee determines that any individual was reidentified or that it is determined that individuals could be reidentified.

Licensors should consider including a right to immediately suspend or terminate a licensee's access to the database in the event the licensor has reason to know or suspect that deidentified individuals were or could be reidentified, thus compromising the database.

Licensees, on the other hand, who do not otherwise intend to try to identify individuals should be concerned that a licensor has provided them with data that does not properly deidentify the datasets, thus putting a licensee at greater risk, such as in the event of a breach. Licensees should consider provisions designed to:

- Ensure that datasets provided are properly deidentified and comply with all applicable privacy and security laws;
- Ensure that the licensor has the necessary rights to use and provide to the licensee the identifiable information, to the extent applicable; and

- Provide the licensee with notice should the licensor discover that information provided is not properly deidentified or that it has reason to believe that such data could be reidentified.

7.6 CONFIDENTIALITY

In addition to the intellectual property rights discussed previously and a well-worded license grant provision, licensors should impose a strong confidentiality obligation on their licensees to ensure the database is held in strict confidence. This is particularly critical to maintain any trade secrets in the database. The license agreement should require the licensee to acknowledge the database and its contents are the confidential information of the licensor and it may not disclose any information made available by the licensor, including the database, unless expressly authorized under the agreement or as otherwise required by law.

To avail itself of the protections of confidentiality, it is not sufficient for a licensor to claim the information as its confidential information. In fact, a licensor must treat such information as its confidential information, which includes employing and requiring the licensee to employ proper physical, administration, and technical safeguards to ensure the confidentiality of such information as well as to prevent the improper disclosure to or access by a third party. Often, this obligation is accomplished through the use of appropriate language in the license agreement. In some cases, licensors include an attachment stating their minimum information security requirements for a licensee to access the licensor's confidential information. Additional limitations may include restrictions on the ability of the licensee to use, disclose, copy, or otherwise make such information available to a third party. As discussed in the trade section, licensees should carefully review any such information security requirements to determine the licensee's ability to comply, the costs of complying, and whether such requirements are appropriate for the nature of the information being protected.

Licensees should consider requiring protection of their own confidential information. Depending on the nature of the engagement, a licensee may provide some of its own confidential information, such as certain data and other information, to the licensor in connection with an audit or otherwise in the performance of the agreement and should expect equal protection for their own confidential information.

Licensors generally restrict a licensee's ability to use, share, and otherwise disclose and make the information available to third parties. In such cases, the licensor may consider the following additional restrictions and obligations with respect to the licensee's ability to grant sublicenses under its license:

- Provides only that information for which it is granted the right to disclose;
- Provides the information only to those authorized parties to whom the licensee is allowed to disclose the information; and
- Requires that any authorized third party with access is subject to obligations of confidentiality no less stringent than those set forth in the agreement between the licensor and the licensee.

Failure to ensure these protections may result in the licensor's (and licensee's, as applicable) loss of protection in the database, its content, and any algorithms associated with it. For example, if the licensor was claiming trade secret protection over a customer list or an algorithm but failed to require the licensee to limit its disclosure of such customer list or algorithm or does not require the recipient to maintain the confidentiality of such information, then it would be reasonable to conclude that a court would find that the owner of the trade secret, customer list or algorithm failed to take adequate protection, thus denying the owner protection of such customer list or algorithm.

7.7 SALTING THE DATABASE

"Salting" a database is a common technique used by licensors to protect their database and detect unauthorized copying. It refers to seasoning the database with dummy or fake data that is difficult, if not impossible, to detect by others. Consider use of salting in the context of the example given regarding copyright protection for a telephone book. Because the telephone book comprises information entirely available publicly, if a competitor of the publisher of the telephone book publishes an identical listing of names and numbers, it would be difficult to prove the competitor simply copied the original book. But, if the original had been salted and one of those fake addresses showed up in the competitor's book, it would be clear that the competitor copied the original book. This same principle can be applied to almost any form of database. The larger the database, the more difficult it would be for a third party to detect and remove the salted data.

A public example of salting a database was when Google started to suspect that Microsoft was copying the results of Google's search engine to improve the results of Microsoft's own Bing search engine. In an effort to confirm its suspicion, Google began to insert fake search results into its search engine and enlisted several engineers to run specific searches using Google via Microsoft's Internet Explorer browser and enabled certain settings in the browser that sent information back to Microsoft. Soon thereafter, when running the same search on Bing, Bing began to return the same fake search results as Google. Google went public, claiming that Microsoft copied the search results and provided examples, including the use of the fake search results planted by Google.[3]

7.8 TERMINATION

Licensors generally seek broad rights of termination with respect to Big Data license agreements. In particular, licensors typically seek the right to terminate the license agreement because:

- Of the licensee's use of the licensed data in excess of the rights granted under the agreement;
- The licensor knows or suspects that deidentified individuals were or could be reidentified; or
- Of the licensee's breach of any of the privacy and security standards.

Licensees generally also seek broad termination rights in order to minimize their liability given that data license agreements generally have little to protect a licensee if, for example, the database is found to be unreliable or outdated, or becomes the subject of an infringement claim. In particular, licensees generally should consider the ability to terminate the license agreement because:

- The data becomes the subject of an intellectual property infringement claim;
- The licensee knows or has reason to believe that the licensor does not have the necessary rights or consents as required by the terms of the

agreement or as necessary in order for the licensee to fully exploit the database as provided for under the agreement; and

- Of the licensee's convenience.

The last licensee termination right is often heavily negotiated, but it is often the licensee's best defense against poor performance or poor-quality data. It also enables the licensor to walk away from an engagement where there is no perceived value or the licensee is no longer interested in the particular database.

7.9 FEES/ROYALTIES

7.9.1 Revenue Models

Typically, a licensee will provide some form of compensation to a licensor for regular access to a database. However, the traditional means of compensation may not be the best approach for Big Data licensing given the differences in how the traditional, structured databases are valued and how Big Data is valued. In fact, setting rates for access to Big Data might be one of the most distinct differences between the traditional data license agreement and the data license agreement for access to Big Data.

Mining for value in Big Data is much like mining for gold. Both have the potential for significant value that is waiting to be discovered. Both require substantial investment, time, and resources to discover the wealth hidden in all the rubble. Many lured by the prospect of hitting it rich invested all they had in the hopes of striking gold. Unfortunately, for every story of someone who struck gold, there are multitudes of stories of those who invested everything and found nothing. Big Data mining is not much different. It can be resource intensive and costly and take a fair amount of time. To truly unlock the value of Big Data, the cost of entry may need to be lowered. However, if the cost of entry is not set properly, there will be a disincentive for the collectors and purveyors of Big Data to continue collecting it and making it available to others. Therefore, in creating new models for Big Data licensing, one must ensure that any lowering of the cost of entry must be designed so it does not sacrifice a licensor's ability to profit and continue to invest and grow its database.

Consideration for the cost of entry is critical. It must be low enough that there are new licensees joining the ecosystem on a regular basis, yet high enough to ensure the licensors are rewarded for their investment. Licensees and licensors are at odds regarding how this should be accomplished. Licensees claim that mining Big Data is inconclusive, and the value has not yet been proven. As a result, some licensees avoid paying for access to Big Data and prefer to retain a consultant to advise on trends and other speculative matters or seek out other alternatives for gathering information. Although there have been many success stories regarding Big Data, generally licensors lack sufficient data points to determine the value in the large, unproven, ever-changing datasets.

Accordingly, other compensation models need to be considered. One approach is to liken of the speculative value of Big Data with that of certain early-stage, speculative patent and know-how licenses for research and development and other development purposes. In this case, a licensee would enter into a license agreement to gain access to certain information and intellectual property with the hope of turning that information into commercial value. Under such an arrangement, fees take the form of a low, up-front payment, with future royalties tied to the ability of the licensee to commercialize the intellectual property and know-how. In some cases, milestone payments are also included to ensure the licensee continues to develop the licensed intellectual property and not let it sit. The greater the value the licensee created or was able to extract, the greater the fees payable to the licensor, thus allowing the licensor to enable a low-risk cost of entry for the licensee yet maintain the ability to extract return from the licensed material.

Following this example, licensors of Big Data may wish to consider a relatively low up-front, initial fee to provide greater access to the data and to expand to a potentially greater pool of licensees. This can be tied to certain interim or minimum periodic payments to ensure the licensee continues to seek new commercial or internal value and properly incentivize the licensee to engage in productive use. Given the lower initial costs, the license grant should be tied to the ability of a licensor to receive royalties based on the extracted value or such other metric that is tied to the extracted or mined value.

Setting the fees in this manner may eliminate discussions between the parties regarding determination of the value of the licensed data as well as the typical argument that each party is under- or overvaluing the value of the database.

Another concern licensors have is how to ensure a licensee does not cannibalize the licensor's ability to extract value by licensing access to the database to other parties. In some cases, licensees seek to monetize their own investment or lower the cost of access by turning around and granting sublicenses. The royalty scheme proposed herein would easily allow a licensee, subject to proper protections, to grant sublicenses without a licensor fearing loss of potential revenue. In this particular case, the licensee's sublicensing of the database would represent a commercial value, of which the licensor would be entitled to compensation in the form of a royalty. Thus, depending on the nature of the database and the licensees, allowing the licensee to grant further licenses under this model would not cannibalize the licensor's potential revenue stream associated with the database.

7.9.2 Price Protection

Once the license agreement is entered into, a licensee will lose significant leverage when it comes to price protection. Accordingly, a licensee should negotiate price protections when entering into the relationship. In particular, licensees should require a period of fixed fees, such as during the initial term of the license agreement, during which the licensor will be prohibited from raising the licensee's rates. The licensor may, however, increase the rates at the start of a renewal period, subject to adequate prior written notice and the amount of such increase is capped at an amount equal to the percentage change in the Consumer Price Index (CPI) during the preceding calendar year and 4%, whichever is less.

It is not uncommon for licensors to claim licensees owe additional fees, such as fees for access to additional databases, sharing in the cost of network storage devices, and software required to access, process, and analyze the databases. Accordingly, it is critical that a licensee includes a statement that unless otherwise stated in writing and signed by the licensee, there are no other fees to be paid by the licensee in connection with the agreement.

7.10 AUDIT

Licensors should always consider including an audit in their license agreements permitting them (or a third-party auditor designated by the licensor) to inspect the licensee's records and systems to confirm that the licensee's use of the database complies with the scope of the licensee's authorized use under the license agreement. In addition to the right to enter and inspect the licensee's facilities and systems, it is important for licensors to require the licensee to properly maintain its books and records regarding its use of the database. These records should be kept throughout the term of the license agreement as well as for an appropriate period of time after the termination or expiration of the license agreement. Audits should cover the licensee's use of the database, as well as the licensee's security used to protect and secure the database or access thereto. This is a critical right designed to ensure protection of the licensor's data. In the event the audit reveals noncompliance, it is typical for the costs of the audit to shift to the licensee and that the licensee be responsible for additional license fees to compensate the licensor for any excess use of the data. Depending on the nature of information licensed, some licensors have sought to include an indemnification directly within the audit provision. In addition to any other rights a licensor may have, including with respect to the right to seek indemnification under the license agreement, licensors may require a licensee to indemnify the licensor against any claims that may arise relating to the licensee's compliance as determined by the audit. Even if the licensor never exercises its audit right, the threat is frequently sufficient to ensure licensee compliance with the terms of the agreement.

From the licensee's perspective, audit rights can be problematic. Licensors have been known to abuse the audit process, conducting highly invasive audits that disrupt the licensee's operations. Language should be added to the license agreement limiting the number of audits that can be conducted in a given period of time (e.g., once in any 12-month period) and making clear any audit must be conducted so as not to unreasonably interfere with or disrupt the licensee's business. Licensees may also want to consider restricting a licensor's ability to take multiple attempts at uncovering a licensee's noncompliance by preventing a licensor from reauditing records that were previously audited and found to be compliant.

Because audits will almost certainly expose the licensor to confidential information of the licensee, the license agreement should include an appropriate confidentiality provision. If the licensee is a regulated entity, the licensee should consider refusing any on-site audit rights and limiting the audit to off-site review of the licensee's records.

In some cases, the licensor may engage a third-party auditor whose compensation is based on whether it finds noncompliance. This type of compensation arrangement can create an adversarial relationship between the auditor and the licensee. Licensees should consider including language in the audit clause precluding such compensation arrangements.

Because the cost of the audit typically shifts to the licensee in the event noncompliance is found, licensees should revise the audit provision to ensure those fees do not become excessive. Although it is common to include language such as "fees must be reasonable," this is frequently not enough. A better approach is to include language preventing the fees from the audit from exceeding some specified percentage of the noncompliance (e.g., "The costs of the audit shall not exceed 25% of the amount of any underpayment by the Licensee"). In this example language, if the licensee has used the database such that additional license fees of $10,000 are due, the amount of the audit costs may not exceed $2,500.00.

7.11 WARRANTY

Big Data is merely a collection of large datasets, often unverified and unchecked. Although the licensor may have created some of the licensed data, given the complexity and size of the Big Data databases, it is unlikely that all data contained therein was generated by the licensor and even less likely that one is able to verify the data. As such, licensors generally provide the database on an "as-is" basis and therefore are unlikely to agree to any protection with respect to a licensee's use of the data, any errors in the data, or losses resulting from the use of the data. However, many of these provisions will likely depend on the actual data licensed.

One common theme often repeated by many licensors is that Big Data is provided or made available to others as a research tool. Generally, research tools are made available at the licensee's discretion and advisement. The licensee is therefore generally responsible for determining the applicability and legality of the use of the dataset and any results in its sole and absolute discretion. Therefore, any losses or liabilities incurred by the licensee based on any action or inaction taken by the licensee, as between the licensor and the licensee, are those of the licensee.

Under a traditional license agreement, the licensor was often asked to warrant that:

- it was the owner or licensee (with the right to sublicense to others) of the data it was licensing;

- it owned or had the necessary rights and consents to grant access to the data to the licensee; and
- the licensee's intended use of the data is allowable.

However, with Big Data, given the vast amounts and variety of data within the licensed database and the variety of ways in which such data is collected, it is difficult to know with any certainty the nature and scope of data contained therein or what rights a licensor may have in the licensed data. Accordingly, licensees may express some caution when entering into agreements granting access to Big Data, especially where licensors are hesitant and even unwilling to provide certain warranties that licensees are accustomed to receiving under typical software and even some database licensing agreements.

Stemming from the traditional data license agreements, licensees often attempt to pressure licensors into providing (additional) warranties with respect to the nature of the database. However, even traditional "acceptable" data license warranties are somewhat problematic for licensors of Big Data. Typical warranties that may be found in a standard data license agreement may include:

- The licensor has all rights necessary, including those of third parties, in order to grant the rights provided under the agreement;
- (To the best of its knowledge as of the effective date), licensee's authorized use of the data does not and shall not infringe the rights of any third party; and
- The licensed data (to the best of licensor's knowledge) does not contain any errors, and that licensor will promptly notify licensee of such errors and will promptly resolve any such errors in the licensed data.

Although these warranties may be considered reasonable for a typical structured data license, licensors should approach such warranties with caution when dealing with Big Data. Given how the data is collected, the nature of the data, how it is and what is combined with the data, general principles of intellectual property rights, consents granted by individuals whose data was collected, and applicable privacy policies in effect when the information was collected, granting any of these warranties may be highly problematic for a licensor, potentially subjecting the licensor to significant liability. Further complicating this issue is the fact that, in many cases, the licensor did not collect or generate the data being licensed but is merely a licensee itself from a third party. In some cases, a licensor may only be providing access to a third party's database. In each case, the licensor may not have been granted equivalent warranties from its upstream licensors. Thus, it may not be reasonable to expect a licensor to take on the liability belonging to other parties.

Licensees should consider the nature of the license, the nature of the database, and the intended purposes of the license agreement and determine whether certain warranties would be applicable. The following series of warranties may be applicable for licensees of Big Data:

- Licensor, to the best of their knowledge, has the necessary rights to provide or otherwise make the data available to the licensee;
- Licensor is not providing any data to the licensee where licensor knows, or should reasonably know, that they do not have the rights to provide such data; and
- The licensed data has not been manipulated by the licensor or other parties in such a manner as to render the data or the results of any analytics performed on such data questionable or worthless.

The final warranty just presented relates to the issue of data compression and salting of the database. Licensees should consider obtaining some reassurances that the data they are licensing has some value and is not missing potentially key bits of information or does not contain an amount of dummy data significant enough to render the database worthless. Given the size of Big Data, it is not uncommon for licensors to employ the use of lossy compression (i.e., a form of compression by which some of the original information is lost to reduce file size). Licensees should question the licensor on their use of such lossy compression and the use of dummy data. Although licensors are generally willing to discuss the use of compression mechanisms, many are not willing to discuss how, or even whether, they salt their database for fear of circumventing one of their intellectual property protections. Understanding this will enable their licensee to better determine the value of the Big Data licensed. In such instances, some licensees have been able to obtain warranties that any compression techniques applied will be lossless, enabling the licensee to reconstruct data in its original form.

Additional warranties that licensees may wish to consider with respect to the licensing of Big Data include warranties whereby the licensor warrants that:

- The data is not corrupt;
- The licensor did not insert malicious code; and
- With respect to any "structured data," the database is organized and formatted in a particular manner (which is disclosed to the licensee).

7.12 INDEMNIFICATION

An *indemnification* is a contractual provision in which a party (the "indemnitor" or "indemnifying party") promises to pay the losses and other damages incurred by the other party (the "indemnitee" or "indemnified party") under certain conditions as set forth in the agreement. The most common form of indemnification found in license agreements is an indemnity for claims by a third party that the licensed materials infringe that third party's intellectual property rights (e.g., the data in a database was copied without authorization from a third party and that copy infringes the third party's copyrights). Similarly, it is common for the licensor to require an indemnity from the licensee protecting the licensor from claims and damages arising from the licensee's use of the licensed materials in excess of the rights granted in the license agreement (e.g., the licensee is granted a license to use a database for its internal purposes but breaches the license by distributing the database to others, causing an infringement or other type of claim).

Given the nature of Big Data, the unanticipated uses of Big Data, and the risks and liabilities associated with the use and licensing of Big Data discussed in this book, most licensors of Big Data are hesitant or refuse to offer any form of indemnification to a licensee. Licensees have been able to achieve certain protection and/or indemnification given a variety of factors, including as a result of the licensee's negotiating power, the relationship between the parties, and the experience level of the counsel and business team representing the licensor and licensee.

In some instances, a licensee may be well positioned for receipt of limited indemnification. In some cases, licensees and licensors enter into a license agreement for specific reasons, including with respect to specialized Big Data sets. Accordingly, it is not uncommon to receive a limited indemnification, generally subject to a cap on damages, that the licensor has all necessary rights and consents in the licensed database governing the licensed use and sublicense granted to licensee thereunder. In addition, the indemnification may expressly exclude, where appropriate, the delivery of the data and any technology, manipulation, alteration, or combination of the data.

7.13 LIMITATION OF LIABILITY

Almost every license agreement includes a limitation of liability defining the parties' respective liability for damages. Limitations of liability typically have two parts: a disclaimer of all consequential damages (e.g., lost profits) and a cap on all other damages, which is typically linked to some portion of the contract. Licensors generally present a one-sided limitation of liability that protects the licensor and exposes the licensee to unlimited damages. This is common and frequently accepted by licensees.

Licensees generally request two types of changes to the limitation of liability: first that it be made mutual and second that, at minimum, the licensor's confidentiality and indemnity obligations, if any, be excluded from all limitations of liability. If a licensor is inclined to grant mutuality, it must ensure that breach of the license grant or infringement of the licensor's intellectual property rights by the licensee be excluded from the limitation of liability. Without those exclusions, the licensor has essentially sold its rights in the database for the value of the cap on damages. That is, if the agreement disclaims all liability for consequential damages and caps liability at one month of license fees and that language is made mutual, the licensor has just "sold" its rights in the database for one month of fees.

7.14 CONCLUSION

Although there are similarities between traditional license agreements and those used for Big Data, the key differences and issues highlighted in this chapter make clear that using a traditional license agreement is not appropriate for this new type of transaction. Big Data requires a fresh look at common provisions such as intellectual property ownership, indemnification, and the type and scope of license granted. Licensees and licensors can use this chapter as a checklist to mitigate risk in their Big Data license agreements.

NOTES

1. Pub. L. No. 104-191, § 264 (1996), codified at 42 USC § 1320d; Standards for Privacy of Individually Identifiable Health Information, 45 CFR § 160 (2002), 45 CFR § 164 subpts. A, E (2002).
2. 27 CFR Part 248.
3. Danny Sullivan. Google: Bing Is Cheating, Copying Our Search Results. February 1, 2011. http://searchengineland.com/google-bing-is-cheating-copying-our-search-results-62914.

8

The Antitrust Laws and Big Data[*]

*Alan D. Rutenberg, Howard W. Fogt,
and Benjamin R. Dryden*

8.1 INTRODUCTION

The purpose of the antitrust laws is to promote competition between market participants. The laws originally arose in the late 1800s as a response to abuses in the railroad, steel, and energy industries. Since that time, however, the antitrust laws have been steadily revisited and refined through judicial interpretation, legislative amendments, and government enforcement to better fit the needs of an evolving economy. In this way, a body of laws that arose from practices in the nineteenth-century railroad, steel, and energy industries is still used to address practices in twenty-first-century businesses, such as the use of Big Data in decision making.

Big Data represents a new frontier for antitrust. By giving firms a tremendous amount of insight into the actions of their competitors, Big Data, when used properly, can be a powerful, procompetitive tool that allows quicker and more intelligent responses to supply-and-demand conditions. However, when used improperly, Big Data can also provide an opportunity for businesses to send signals to their competitors and to monitor their competitors' reactions to these signals—giving rise to significant risks of tacit price-fixing.

[*] We would like to express our appreciation for the significant contributions to this chapter by the following members of Foley & Lardner LLP's Antitrust Practice Group: Gregory N. Neppl, a partner in the firm's Washington, D.C., office, and Michael A. Naranjo, a senior counsel in the firm's San Francisco office.

115

In this chapter, you will

- Receive a short primer on the antitrust laws;
- Read about specific areas of the antitrust laws implicated by Big Data, including
  - Price-fixing
  - Signaling
  - Information sharing
  - Customizing prices
- Receive recommendations on how to address the antitrust risks that arise in using Big Data to monitor competitors

8.2 OVERVIEW OF THE ANTITRUST LAWS

More than 125 countries around the world regulate antitrust conduct and impose increasingly strict and significant penalties on conduct that restrain competition. Among the most significant regulatory regimes are those in the United States and the European Union. The antitrust laws govern a wide range of business practices. They regulate unilateral conduct, such as monopolization or abuse of a dominant position, as well as horizontal and vertical multiparty conduct that relates to pricing, distribution, and other practices. The antitrust laws also extensively regulate mergers and acquisitions of actual and potential competitors and those involving vertical integration.

The antitrust laws of the United States and the European Union evaluate the legality of business conduct among two or more parties by asking two initial questions. First, the laws ask whether a firm's conduct is so facially anticompetitive (so likely to harm competition) that, as a matter of law, the practice should be condemned automatically without consideration of the practice's potential procompetitive benefits. Practices such as agreements among competitors to fix prices, allocate customers, or divide territories are deemed to be so pernicious that they are condemned as per se illegal, without further inquiry of any possible competitive benefits.

If, however, an activity among parties is not per se illegal, then US and EU regulators ask a second question focusing on the overall competitive effects of the practices.[1] This question is referred to in shorthand as the "rule-of-reason" analysis. Under the rule-of-reason analysis, the antitrust laws ask whether a given trade practice's anticompetitive effect substantially outweighs its procompetitive effect. Among the factors relevant to this analysis are the following: (1) Does the practice potentially facilitate collusion or create market power? (2) Does the practice produce positive competitive benefits such as increased efficiency? and, important, (3) Can the same positive benefits of the practice be achieved in a less restrictive way? If a given trade practice fails the rule-of-reason test, then it is illegal under the antitrust laws.

Case Study 8.1: The Rule of Reason

Applying the rule of reason is often a highly fact-specific exercise. Group purchasing arrangements are one example of the type of conduct traditionally evaluated under a rule-of-reason analysis. Such arrangements are different in kind than the type of facially anticompetitive conduct that is subject to per se condemnation (such as price-fixing among competitors on bids or other customer sales). Although group purchasing programs typically involve price-related agreements in that the organization negotiates prices with vendors on behalf of its members, such restraints often are reasonably necessary for an integrated group purchasing venture to achieve efficiencies that members would not be able to achieve individually.

Group purchasing arrangements are common and often are a procompetitive, lawful way for groups of firms to pool their purchases to lower costs. In analyzing group purchasing arrangements, the courts and the antitrust enforcement agencies also take into consideration two primary potential concerns. One potential concern is whether the combination of purchasers possesses market power on the buying side that would enable the group to depress prices for the purchased products below competitive levels and potentially depress output. Accordingly, it is important to consider what percentage of the sales of a purchased product is made by a group.

The second potential concern is that the buying group may facilitate collusion among its participants through standardizing costs or facilitating the ability of participants to monitor their competitors' production or output levels. Risk is more likely to arise when the purchased product is a large component of the cost of products sold by the members of the group purchasing organization.

8.3 BIG DATA AND PRICE-FIXING

One of the fundamental concerns of the antitrust laws is "price-fixing," or efforts between competitors to reduce price competition. Price-fixing takes many forms and is both a civil violation and a federal crime. In the classic case, price-fixing occurs in a closed-door meeting where a group of competing chief executive officers (in a smoke-filled room, of course) hatch a nefarious plot to stop competing and hike up their prices in unison. Although these cases do happen, modern-day price-fixing cases can involve allegations that two or more companies—without direct proof of the parties ever meeting together or forming an explicit agreement—nevertheless developed a tacit agreement to set their prices close to one another. Such "tacit" price-fixing cases represent the greater challenge for compliance personnel to deter because the line between lawful and unlawful behavior may depend on the intent of those involved.

In this respect, Big Data represents a new frontier for antitrust. By giving firms a tremendous amount of insight into the actions of their competitors, Big Data, when used properly, can be a powerful, procompetitive tool that allows quicker and more intelligent responses to supply-and-demand conditions. However, when used improperly, Big Data can also provide an opportunity for businesses to send signals to their competitors and to monitor their competitors' reactions to these signals—giving rise to significant risks of tacit price-fixing. For these reasons, companies should implement antitrust safeguards and training and consider antitrust risks in using Big Data to monitor one's competitors.

8.4 PRICE-FIXING RISKS

Antitrust authorities have had little occasion to contemplate the legality of using Big Data to set prices or track competitors' actions.[2] However, it is safe to assume that well-established antitrust principles will be brought to bear on any Big Data antitrust case. Agreements to fix prices are illegal per se and may be prosecuted criminally. Under US antitrust law, there can be no price-fixing, however, without an "agreement," either explicit or tacit, between two or more market players. Put in other words, a *unilateral* pricing decision cannot give rise to price-fixing liability.[3] Consequently, neither a "follow-the-leader" strategy nor "conscious parallelism" (by which each seller knowingly matches, but does not beat, its competitor's price) amount to illegal price-fixing as long as the competitors each decide to charge the same prices independently rather than through an agreement.[4]

To illustrate the application of price-fixing concepts, imagine a small town that has two gas stations. Station A updates its prices every Monday at

9:00 a.m. based on market fluctuations, and it posts its prices on a large sign for passing motorists. Every Monday at 9:05 a.m., the manager of Station B drives past Station A to see what prices Station A is charging this week. And, every Monday at 9:06 a.m., Station B decides to charge the exact same price as Station A. The townsfolk might be understandably suspicious of this behavior. However, as long as this pricing is based on purely independent decision making, it is legal under the antitrust laws. Station B might have legitimate, self-interested motivations for matching Station A's prices; for instance, Station B might believe that Station A has superior insight into supply-and-demand conditions than Station B has. Therefore, as long as Station A and Station B each act independently in reaching their pricing decisions, then the mere fact that they charge the same prices is not illegal. But, by the same token, if Station B follows Station A's prices based on so much as a tacit agreement between the parties—for example, a wordless nod[5] exchanged between the managers creating an agreement—then both stations are at risk for a criminal price-fixing conspiracy and may be liable for treble damages for the above-market pricing that results.

In the Big Data context, then, a bright line separates legal conduct from illegal conduct, but the opportunities for a wayward employee to cross that bright line are many. The bright line is this: A company has substantial leeway to employ legal methods to unilaterally collect information about its competitors and to use this information to set its own prices. Thus, companies have wide discretion to collect and analyze proprietary, public, or purchased data to try to ascertain their competitors' prices, costs, margins, volumes, or other sensitive information.[6] Developing such intelligence has great potential to enhance a company's ability to react to supply-and-demand conditions, and the antitrust laws encourage such enterprising, procompetitive behavior. Similarly, companies should feel free to use such analyses to set their own prices or output.

This expanded knowledge of one's competitors' behavior, however, comes with significant risks for abuse. If two competing factories each have extensive, real-time knowledge of each other's prices, then a constant opportunity is created for the two firms to come to a tacit agreement to fix prices. For example, imagine if Factory A raises its price for a specific widget to $100, and Factory B follows; Factory A then raises its prices to $105, and Factory B follows; and then Factory A finally raises its price to $110, and Factory B follows. Although independent decisions on pricing are permissible, if the two firms' ability to monitor one another's prices leads them to come to an agreement to adhere to one another's prices, then they are price-fixing. Further, parallel conduct combined with other circumstantial evidence (such as taking actions that would be against a party's self-interest in the absence of any agreement) may be used as evidence to prove a price-fixing agreement.

The great difficulty for in-house compliance personnel is that the line between legal and illegal conduct in this situation may turn on the intent of the price setters. Moreover, even if no "agreement" is ever actually reached, there remains the practical risk that a single careless email about "price stability" or an industry "truce" might be enough, many years after the fact, to convince a jury otherwise. Thus, although Big Data carries great promise to allow firms to legally analyze competitors and set prices based on this knowledge, Big Data also carries a great practical risk for abuse. And, perhaps a more practical concern is that Big Data also may increase the risk of an expensive investigation, lawsuit, or jury verdict, even when a company is not price-fixing at all.

In addition, once a price-fixing conspiracy is in place, Big Data can make it much easier for the parties (at this point, called a "cartel") to perpetuate the conspiracy. As a practical matter, many price-fixing cartels dissolve not because of law enforcement but rather because the economic incentives for a cartel member to "cheat" by underselling the rest of the cartel are so compelling.[7] Big Data, however, can give cartels a mechanism through which to monitor their members' pricing. By giving each conspirator insight into its coconspirators' prices and volumes, the cartel can ensure that each member is sticking to the plan and thereby preserve honor among thieves. Should a member of the conspiracy attempt to cheat, the remaining coconspirators might attempt to discipline the cheater by offering short-term fire-sale prices to show the cheater what would happen if the conspiracy fell apart. Thus, Big Data not only enhances the risks of entering into a price-fixing conspiracy in the first place but also, by facilitating such "policing," increases the likelihood that a given conspiracy will survive for a long time.

8.5 "SIGNALING" RISKS

Price-fixing requires an agreement, whether explicit or tacit, with a competitor. However, even if unilateral conduct does not amount to price-fixing, antitrust liability can nevertheless attach for unilateral efforts to try to induce a price-fixing agreement. Under various legal theories, the

US Department of Justice and Federal Trade Commission (DOJ/FTC) have successfully brought "invitation to collude" or "signaling" cases against both companies and individuals alike. For example, invitation-to-collude cases have been brought for calling a competitor's CEO to propose a price-fixing conspiracy (to which the competing CEO responded by refusing the conspiracy and handing a tape of the call over to the Federal Bureau of Investigation)[8] and for announcing plans to limit competition on public earnings conference calls when the company knew its competitors would be listening.[9] In addition, private plaintiffs have used state fair trade acts, which are modeled on the federal antitrust laws, to challenge similar conduct.[10] In short, even if an actual agreement to fix prices is never reached, a deliberate, unilateral attempt to signal toward price-fixing can nevertheless give rise to antitrust liability.

To give an example of an invitation-to-collude case, referring to the previous example of a small town with two gas stations, imagine if a third gas station (Station C) decided to open shop in the town. Assume that right before Station C's opening, the manager of Station A issued a press release saying that if any station in town tries to undercut Station A's prices, then Station A will aggressively cut its own prices. The press release goes on to state that if competitors simply match Station A's prices, then the town will be big enough for all three stations, and they will be able to coexist. In that case, both Station A and its manager could find themselves at risk for antitrust liability for inviting the other players in the market to collude with Station A.

Just as important, this signaling activity by Station A could also be used as circumstantial evidence to support a theory that Station A and Station B had been price-fixing all along—even years before the newspaper story was ever run.[11] If a lawsuit were filed against the stations, this signaling behavior by Station A might be enough to convince a jury that Station A and Station B's previous years of parallel pricing behavior had not really been independent. Therefore, Station A and Station B could face protracted, expensive litigation and potentially significant liability, even though their pricing behavior to date had been perfectly independent and legal.

In the world of Big Data, companies should consider the new dangers that exist for engaging in price signaling. For example, imagine if Factory A learns or suspects that competing Factory B is using trade association data to try to reverse-engineer Factory A's prices, costs, margins, volumes, or other sensitive information. If Factory A suddenly went out of its way to provide more detailed data to the trade association than ever before in the

ANTITRUST COMPLIANCE POLICY

An antitrust compliance policy is a written document that provides employees with a basic understanding of the antitrust laws and how they affect one's business. Antitrust compliance policies often may be provided to employees during orientation, and it is valuable for employees, particularly those with price-setting, sales and marketing, or strategic decision-making authority, to be periodically reminded to review the policy or provided "refresher" antitrust trainings. Having such a policy in place reduces the risk of an antitrust violation occurring. A good antitrust compliance policy also may help mitigate the fallout in the event of a future investigation.

At a minimum, an antitrust compliance policy should explain the rules governing price-fixing and other dealings with competitors. Depending on the nature of the particular business, an antitrust compliance policy might also cover topics such as setting resale prices, "tying" the sale of two different products, price discrimination (see Section 8.9), or other topics. Employees should also be given practical advice about what sort of language to use in internal and external documents (for example, "Do not use exaggerations such as 'dominating the market' or 'destroying the competition'"). Finally, it is helpful for the policy to advise employees about how to behave when meeting with competitors, such as in social settings or at trade association meetings.

hopes that Factory B would use this new data to bring its prices in line with Factory A's, then Factory A may risk being charged with signaling. This risk exists even if Factory B never ends up following Factory A's prices.

8.6 STEPS TO REDUCE PRICE-FIXING AND SIGNALING RISKS

It bears repeating that Big Data carries great potential to improve individual firms' abilities to respond to supply-and-demand conditions, and the antitrust laws absolutely encourage this procompetitive, efficiency-enhancing behavior. However, because Big Data also poses risks for abuse, companies should take reasonable steps to ensure that Big Data is only put toward its permissible ends.

First, companies should make sure that their employees have a basic understanding of the antitrust laws. Employee training should include familiarizing oneself with the company's antitrust compliance policy, and periodic compliance "refresher" trainings should include discussions of antitrust laws. Such antitrust training is particularly important for employees who have authority over pricing, sales and marketing, and strategic decisions.

Moreover, as companies roll out Big Data initiatives, companies should consider having employees undertake specialized antitrust training before being permitted to access sensitive data about competitors' prices, costs, margins, volumes, or other sensitive information. This training should include not only a reminder that it is unlawful to fix prices, but also best practices for document creation. A casual email by a relatively low-level sales manager may be the critical document in a price-fixing or signaling case[12]; therefore, it is important that employees understand not only the legal pitfalls of Big Data use but also the practical consequences of using inaccurate or overly optimistic language even in casual documents.

Second, if appropriate, companies should consider erecting firewalls between those individuals who have access to raw data and those individuals who have price-setting or strategic decision-making authority. For instance, in certain cases it may be advisable for a data analyst or even an outside consultant to be retained to process raw competitive data into an aggregated or anonymous format, such that the business decision makers may use the data for necessary and proper ends but not for unnecessary or improper ones. Similarly, in certain cases it may be advisable for datasets and reports to be cleansed of formulas and other metadata before being shared with business decision makers to ensure that only the necessary information is shared. Companies also should consider the propriety of using competitive data collected by an affiliate or other division. For instance, a company may be a supplier to competitors of another sister company, and it can be advisable to put in place appropriate firewalls so that this business relationship is not viewed as facilitating potential coordination among the competing entities.

Even assuming a company is careful not to communicate with competitors and only to collect information from acceptable third-party sources, it is a good practice to track the sources of the data it obtains about its competitors and to document how such data is incorporated into strategic decisions. For instance, without an internal note that a company received a competitor's price list from a customer while negotiating a contract with the customer, there is a risk that a judge or jury may assume that the price list came from the competitor. Plaintiffs' attorneys have argued that the mere presence of a competitor's price list in a defendant's possession serves as circumstantial evidence that a price-fixing conspiracy existed between the defendant and the competitor. Although courts have often rejected such arguments,[13] only time will tell how a jury would react to a company possessing detailed records of its competitor's costs, volumes, margins, and other sensitive information. Therefore, to minimize the risks that these reports might represent in future litigation, companies should take steps to document the source of each such report. Take, for instance, a report that estimates a competing firm's prices. A simple footnote on the first page of that report explaining that the information was derived from an internal analysis of the August 7, 2015, XYZ database might make a significant difference in a litigation where a plaintiff argues that the report is, instead, evidence of a price-fixing agreement with the competitor.

Similarly (and assuming that a company is not actually in a price-fixing conspiracy with its competitors), to the extent that competitive analyses are used in making strategic decisions, it will be valuable to document the nature of their use. For instance, a two-sentence footnote explaining that a given analysis was used to help the company come in at a lower price than a competitor or to soften a planned price increase could prove extremely helpful in a future litigation to dispel a claim that the analysis was instead used to fix prices.

8.7 INFORMATION-SHARING RISKS

An additional antitrust risk related to Big Data arises from the fact that an agreement to exchange certain types of information—wholly apart from an agreement to fix prices—may itself be actionable under the antitrust laws. Referring once again to the example of the competing factories (A and B), imagine if these two competitors were to exchange information concerning their pricing, outputs, or markets as part of a trade association that also included competing factories C and D. Access to such strategic information creates an opportunity for these competitors to come to an unlawful agreement concerning prices or the allocation of markets.

Even if an agreement never is reached, the fact that strategic information has been exchanged invites scrutiny by regulators as well as potentially costly litigation.[14] Indeed, an illegal agreement can be inferred from the exchange of information and subsequent market conduct that is inconsistent with free and independent competition.

Unlike an agreement among competitors to fix prices, which is thought to have no possible redeeming virtues and accordingly is illegal per se, agreements simply to exchange information are understood to be potentially beneficial to competition and therefore are judged under the rule of reason.[15] Under the rule of reason, courts and enforcement agencies consider whether the anticompetitive harm of the information exchange outweighs the procompetitive benefits of the exchange, and the exchange is only found unlawful if its harm outweighs its benefits. Because rule-of-reason violations are fact intensive, they do not carry the risk of criminal penalties; they do, however, carry significant civil risks.

In general, the antitrust risk posed by information exchanges directly correlates with how likely it is that the information being shared can be used to undermine competition. Various factors may raise the antitrust risks posed by information exchange programs, including the market concentration of the industry in question; the nature of the information involved (does it relate to prices, inventories, or costs?); the level of aggregation (is the data sufficiently masked to prevent identification of individual competitors?); the age of the data when it was disseminated (is it historic or forward looking?); whether other industry characteristics facilitate effective collusion among market participants (e.g., the commodity nature of a product or pricing transparency); and industry structures tending to stabilize or raise prices or restrict output (e.g., ownership links or alliances among competitors). The justification for the exchange, naturally, is also important.

All else being equal, agreements to exchange price, output, costs, or strategic planning information are far more likely to be challenged than, say, agreements to exchange technical information or know-how. Similarly, agreements to exchange information about current or projected market conditions are more likely to be challenged than agreements to exchange historical information, and agreements to exchange information about individual companies are more likely to be challenged than agreements to exchange aggregated information that merely describes the broader market.[16] Furthermore, the existence of a highly concentrated market (e.g., four or fewer producers dominating the market) or industry characteristics that facilitate collusion increase the antitrust risks posed by an information exchange program.

Unfortunately, there is no consistent set of rules that can be relied on to ensure low or no risk. The world of Big Data is global, and there are sometimes conflicting rules that require consideration in distinguishing lawful information exchanges from unlawful ones. In the United States, for example, the DOJ/FTC issued guidelines for collaborations among competitors in 2000, but these only speak in general terms about the relevant considerations that bear on whether an information exchange is permissible.[17] The only US bright lines that exist are "safety zones" for information exchanges in the health care sector. These safety zones are contained in guidelines that the DOJ/FTC adopted in 1996, and they have not been updated since. In these US health care guidelines, which also have been looked to for guidance in non-health-care contexts, the agencies have stated that they will not challenge information exchanges among health care providers as long as five conditions are met:

1. The collection must be managed by a third party such as a government agency, consultant, or trade association;
2. Any fee-, price-, or wage-related information must be more than three months old;
3. At least five providers must participate in the exchange;
4. No individual provider's data may represent more than 25% of the total data on a weighted basis; and
5. "Any information disseminated is sufficiently aggregated such that it would not allow recipients to identify the prices charged or compensation paid by any individual provider."[18]

Although these guidelines do not have the force of law and merely represent a safety zone from government enforcement, at least one court has cited them as persuasive authority of the bounds of permissible exchange in a price-fixing case.[19] Therefore, the health care guidelines are increasingly regarded as informative guidance for information exchanges in other contexts and industries.

In contrast to the United States, the European Commission in 2011 issued seemingly much more restrictive information-sharing guidelines.[20] These EU guidelines are much less explicit and more amorphous than the 2000 DOJ/FTC guidelines and are much more rigorous than the 1996 health care guidelines. The European Commission advises that an "information exchange can constitute a concerted practice if it reduces strategic uncertainty in the market thereby facilitating collusion, that is to say, if the data exchanged is strategic."[21] The European Commission provides further guidance:

- For an information exchange to have an appreciable effect on competition, it must be likely to have an appreciable adverse impact on one of the several parameters of competition, such as price, output, product quality, product variety, or innovation.
- Whether an exchange of information will have restrictive effects on competition depends on both the economic conditions of the relevant markets and the characteristics of the information exchanged.
- The exchange of information may change the market conditions in such a way that coordination becomes possible after the exchange—for example, by increasing transparency in a market, reducing market complexity, buffering instability, or compensating for asymmetry.[22]
- Antitrust risk is heightened "in markets which are sufficiently transparent, concentrated, non-complex, stable and symmetric."[23]

In short, EU antitrust regulators would likely see many information exchanges as increasing market transparency, reducing market complexity, buffering instability, and compensating for asymmetry. For such a regulator, these are negatives. Although the European Commission acknowledges that, in certain circumstances, information exchanges may lead to efficiency gains and may allow companies to make better investment decisions and to better allocate capital resources toward growing markets, such exchanges must be properly structured to avoid being viewed as facilitating collusion.[24] Unlike the US rules, there are even fewer bright lines, even on such basic questions like what constitutes "historic" data (generally at least one year depending on the commercial realities of the particular industry) or "public" information (generally publication is not sufficient unless widely disseminated to all likely consumers).

In the world of Big Data, information sharing is likely to play an increasingly important role in antitrust enforcement. Companies must thoroughly consider antitrust risks before agreeing to exchange databases or data analyses with their competitors or through trade association activities. Evaluation of the risks associated with information exchanges in both the United States and the European Union involves highly fact-specific analyses of the nature of the information involved as well as the industry and market characteristics. It is for this reason that information exchanges are an area for which it is highly advisable to consult with counsel before proceeding. For any given information exchange, it will be critical to articulate a procompetitive business rationale for the exchange, as well as to evaluate who will have access to the information and in what form and what may be the impact on competition from the exchange. This is true not only at the onset of an information exchange program but also on an ongoing basis throughout the life of the program. It is possible that information that historically did not raise antitrust concerns to share may increasingly raise antitrust risk. That risk is especially true in the age of Big Data because of the enhanced ability of parties to access further information and data that may allow them to disaggregate or extrapolate from exchanged information in ways that were not available in the past.

8.8 DATA PRIVACY AND SECURITY POLICIES AS FACETS OF NONPRICE COMPETITION

As noted, the antitrust laws exist to promote competition between market participants. Although price competition is central to this concern, the Supreme Court has made clear that "for antitrust purposes, there is no meaningful distinction between price and non-price components of a transaction."[25] Thus, the antitrust laws serve to promote competition not only for price but also for nonprice interests such as credit terms, quality, product safety, product choice, and convenience. As Big Data plays an ever-larger role in the marketplace, it stands to reason that data privacy and security policies will become an increasingly important nonprice differentiator between competitors. Although no such actions have been brought to date, antitrust regulators have raised the prospect that nonprice competition for data privacy or security policies could play a major role in antitrust enforcement matters in the future.[26]

To illustrate the concern, suppose that an upstart Internet search provider adopted an industry-leading privacy policy that attracted a devoted customer base and won share from larger search providers. If one of the larger search providers then acquired the upstart firm, antitrust regulators likely would be less concerned about the acquisition's potential effect on price competition—because Internet searches are free to consumers—but perhaps more concerned that the acquisition might substantially lessen nonprice competition for privacy practices among search firms. Therefore, in evaluating potential mergers, acquisitions, and joint ventures, companies should be mindful that antitrust regulators may in appropriate cases evaluate the transaction's likely effects on nonprice data policies (as well as other aspects of consumer choice).

Outside the merger context, companies should also be vigilant to avoid anticompetitive agreements with competitors about data privacy or security policies. Companies should not form agreements with their competitors to limit the extent to which they safeguard data privacy or security. For example, the antitrust regulators may be highly skeptical of a trade association adopting industry standards that endorse an unreasonably low level of data security as a best practice.[27] Absent a compelling procompetitive justification for such restriction, such "privacy-fixing" or "security-fixing" may result in an antitrust investigation, challenge, or violation.

That said, just as unilateral action cannot amount to price-fixing, unilateral action also cannot amount to privacy-fixing or security-fixing. If a competitor adopts an unreasonably low level of data security, then one is free to match that low level of security as well—just as long as the decision is made unilaterally rather than through an express or tacit agreement with the competitor.

8.9 PRICE DISCRIMINATION AND THE ROBINSON–PATMAN ACT

One more key commercial promise of Big Data is its potential not only to determine the prices that one's competitors are charging but also to determine the prices that one's prospective customers might be willing to pay. A small amount of geographic, demographic, and purchasing history data about a customer can tell a company a great deal about that customer's willingness to pay a greater or lesser price for a given product. As companies collect more and more data about their customers, therefore, the ability to customize prices for specific customers will become ever more refined. For example, Big Data will increasingly enable a company to determine if Customer A is willing to pay a higher price than Customer B, so that the company can extract the highest possible price from both customers. In addition, Big Data will increasingly enable a company to determine if Customer A is no longer willing to pay the price for a given product that Customer A paid just last week, so that the company can lower its prices in real time to ensure that it keeps Customer A's business. Although it is widely recognized that customizing prices for specific purchasers can be a legitimate, procompetitive business strategy, such "price discrimination" can, in certain circumstances, also be abused.

Therefore, price discrimination is regulated by the antitrust laws, in particular in the United States by the Robinson-Patman Act.[28] The Robinson-Patman Act prohibits sellers from setting different prices between different purchasers of "commodities of like grade and quality," where the effect of such price discrimination "may be substantially to lessen competition or tend to create a monopoly."[29] The Robinson-Patman Act has two broad exceptions: First, sellers may charge reasonable price differences to account for bona fide "differences in the cost of manufacture, sale, or delivery" for different purchasers; and second, otherwise-unlawful price discrimination is allowed where a seller is in good faith meeting an equally low price of a competitor.

Although the FTC has jurisdiction to enforce the Robinson-Patman Act, it rarely does so. Rather, the Robinson-Patman Act is most commonly enforced by private litigants claiming to be the victims of discriminatory pricing. Alleged victims may sue not only the discriminating sellers but also, in certain circumstances, the "favored" buyers who enjoyed the preferential pricing. Although such lawsuits often are not successful on the ultimate merits, they are complex and expensive to litigate to a conclusion. For all these reasons, companies are well advised to consider the Robinson-Patman Act before using Big Data to customize prices for specific purchasers.

An important limitation on the scope of the Robinson-Patman Act is that it only prohibits price discrimination in the sale of "commodities of like grade and quality." Therefore, the sale of intangible services—such as medical services, insurance, and telecommunications services,[30] to name just a few—have been found to fall outside the scope of the Robinson-Patman Act. Similarly, because the Robinson-Patman Act only prohibits price discrimination for the sale of commodities of like grade and quality, sellers of sufficiently customized or otherwise sufficiently differentiated products do not violate the act.[31] Therefore, sellers of intangible services and sellers of sufficiently nonstandard, made-to-order products may use Big Data to develop customized prices for such services without implicating the Robinson-Patman Act.[32]

Even for sellers of Robinson-Patman Act "commodities," however, not all price discrimination is unlawful. Most important, the Robinson-Patman Act only prohibits discriminatory pricing if its effect may be to harm competition or to create a monopoly. Courts have interpreted this language to apply in two basic circumstances: if a seller's discriminatory pricing causes competitive injury to a downstream reseller who has received disfavored pricing[33] or (in extremely rare cases) if a seller "predatorily" prices below its own marginal cost to force a competitor out of business.[34] Therefore, except in the exceedingly rare case in which a firm is targeting competitors by losing money on each sale, the only circumstance in which price discrimination can harm competition is when an upstream business sells a commodity to two resellers at different prices, causing the disfavored reseller (or the disfavored reseller's customers) to lose business to the favored reseller (or to the favored reseller's customers).

In short, retailers and direct-to-consumer manufacturers should not worry about violating the Robinson-Patman Act by using Big Data to customize prices for end users. However, manufacturers and wholesalers that sell commodity products to resellers rather than to end users should be careful not to use Big Data to effect unlawful price discrimination. This is not to say, however, that such companies are prohibited from using Big Data to customize prices altogether. To the contrary, such companies remain free to use Big Data within the confines of the Robinson-Patman Act's exceptions to account for bona fide "differences in the cost of manufacture, sale, or delivery" between purchasers and to identify cases for which it may be necessary to meet the equally low price of a competitor. In fact, for such firms, Big Data may provide an efficient and reliable means of taking full advantage of the Robinson-Patman Act exceptions.

8.10 CONCLUSION

Big Data can be a powerful tool that allows companies to provide quicker and more intelligent responses to supply-and-demand conditions. But, by providing companies significant insight into their competitors, Big Data can also provide an opportunity for companies to unlawfully coordinate such things as prices with their competitors. The potential for such misuse of competitor information means that companies using Big Data should be aware that there are associated antitrust risks. Among other things, companies should consider that:

- More than 125 countries around the world regulate antitrust conduct and impose increasingly strict and significant penalties on conduct that restrains competition.
- Unlawful price-fixing does not require an explicit agreement, and in fact, many price-fixing cases involve tacit agreements.
- A company can be found in violation of the antitrust laws even in the absence of an agreement where there is a unilateral invitation to collude or "signaling."
- Information exchanges among competitors are rife with antitrust risk, and a company should seek the advice of counsel to assist in evaluating the specific circumstances of a particular exchange.
- Even if a company does not engage in unlawful coordination with competitors, the possession of a competitor's strategic information or internal documents with poorly chosen wording (for example, anticompetitive buzzwords) can invite, and make it more costly to defend against, inquiries by regulators and litigation.

However, companies using Big Data to learn more about their competitors and markets can employ various strategies to navigate and help mitigate antitrust risks. Among other things, companies should consider:

- Adopting an antitrust compliance policy that provides employees with a basic understanding of the antitrust laws. By educating employees, the policy may help lessen the risk of an antitrust violation, and the presence of such a policy may help mitigate the fallout from a regulatory investigation.
- Educating employees concerning document creation and, more specifically, avoiding the creation of poorly worded documents that contain negative antitrust buzzwords.
- Documenting the benefits to competition associated with particular uses of competitor information gleaned from Big Data and the source of such competitor information to rebut later allegations that the information was for an inappropriate use or inappropriately obtained.
- Reviewing any potential information-sharing or exchange program with counsel to assess the antitrust risk associated with the program.

NOTES

1. These issues shape the core of the guidelines that enforcement agencies use to evaluate the legal consequences of concerted practices. See, for example, European Commission, Guidelines on the Applicability of Article 101 of the Treaty on the Functioning of the European Union to Horizontal Co-operation Agreements (Guidelines on Horizontal Co-operation Agreements), C 11/1 January 14, 2011; Federal Trade Comm'n and U.S. Dep't of Justice, Antitrust Guidelines for Collaborations Among Competitors 2000.

2. A rare example was posed by *In re Wellpoint, Inc. Out-of-Network "UCR" Rates Litigation*, 903 F. Supp. 2d 880 (C.D. Cal. 2012), where a court considered allegations that various health insurers had conspired to rig a database to artificially reduce the database's calculation of the "usual, customary, and reasonable" rates the insurers were obligated to pay for out-of-network health care services. The plaintiffs' antitrust claims were dismissed for lack of standing, so the court did not reach the merits of the ultimate allegations.

3. See *Bell. Atl. Corp. v. Twombly*, 550 U.S. 544, 553 (2007) ("Because § 1 of the Sherman Act does not prohibit all unreasonable restraints of trade but only restraints effected by a contract, combination, or conspiracy, the crucial question is whether the challenged anticompetitive conduct stems from independent decision or from an agreement, tacit or express"; quotations and citations omitted).

4. See generally *In re Citric Acid Litigation*, 191 F.3d 1090, 1102 (9th Cir. 1999).

5. See *Sunny Hill Farms Dairy Co. v. Kraftco Corp.*, 381 F. Supp. 845, 851 (E.D. Mo. 1974) ("[A]n unlawful agreement can be as ephemeral as a knowing wink"; quotation omitted).

6. See generally *Maple Flooring Manufacturers Ass'n v. United States*, 268 U.S. 563, 583 (1925) ("It was not the purpose or intent of the Sherman Anti-Trust Law to inhibit the intelligent conduct of business operations, nor do we conceive that its purpose was to suppress . . . the individual intelligence of those engaged in commerce, enlightened by accurate information as to the essential elements of the economics of a trade or business. . . . ").

7. See XII Phillip Areeda & Herbert Hovenkamp, Antitrust Law (3d ed. 2012) § 2002(d)(1) ("[W]hen the cartel is producing at equal output and price, each individual cartel member is in a situation that its marginal revenue exceeds its marginal costs—as a result, the cartel member can earn more by producing more, *provided* that other cartel members do not increase their output as well.").

8. *United States v. American Airlines, Inc.*, 743 F.2d 1114 (5th Cir. 1984) (finding conduct actionable as an attempt to monopolize).

9. See Complaint, *In re Valassis Communications*, 141 F.T.C. 247 (2006) (alleging an unfair method of competition in violation of Section 5 of Federal Trade Commission Act).

10. See, for example, *Liu v. Amerco, Inc.*, 677 F.3d 489 (1st Cir. 2012) (allowing invitation to collude case under Massachusetts fair trade act to proceed).

11. See, for example, *Williamson Oil Co. v. Philip Morris USA, Inc.*, 346 F.3d 1287, 1301 (11th Cir. 2003) ("[P]rice fixing plaintiffs must demonstrate the existence of 'plus factors' that . . . render that evidence more probative of conspiracy than of conscious parallelism."); *Burtch v. Milberg Factors, Inc.*, 662 F.3d 212, 227 (3rd Cir. 2011) (examples of such "plus factors" include "(1) evidence that the defendant had a motive to enter into a price fixing conspiracy; (2) evidence that the defendant acted contrary to its interests; and (3) evidence implying a traditional conspiracy").

12. See, for example, Analysis of Agreement Containing Consent Order to Aid Public Comment, *In re U-Haul International, Inc.*, 75 Fed. Reg. 35033, at 35034 (June 21, 2010) (quoting email from regional manager that "I encouraged [a competitor] to monitor my rates and to move their rates up. And they did.").

13. See *In re* Citric Acid Litigation, 191 F.3d 1090, 1103 (9th Cir. 1999).

14. An agreement to exchange pricing information can itself be circumstantial evidence of an agreement to fix prices. For example, if a cartel decided to fix prices at a certain level, then the cartel might also decide to monitor each other's compliance with the price-fixing conspiracy by exchanging sales and pricing information. In such a case, there could be two different violations: the per se unlawful price-fixing conspiracy, as well as an information exchange conspiracy, separately actionable under a "rule-of-reason" challenge.

15. *United States v. United States Gypsum Co.*, 438 U.S. 422, 441 n.16 (1978) ("The exchange of price data and other information among competitors does not invariably have anticompetitive effects; indeed, such practices can in certain circumstances increase economic efficiency and render markets more, rather than less, competitive. For this reason, we have held that such exchanges of information do not constitute a *per se* violation of the Sherman Act.").

16. See generally Federal Trade Comm'n and U.S. Dep't of Justice, Antitrust Guidelines for Collaborations Among Competitors (2000) § 3.31(b).

17. *Id.*

18. U.S. Dep't of Justice and Federal Trade Comm'n, Statements of Antitrust Enforcement Policy in Health Care (1996) §§ 5A-6A.

19. *Cason-Merenda v. Detroit Medical Center*, 862 F. Supp. 2d 603, 630 (E.D. Mich. 2012) ("Yet, rather than relying on such third-party surveys that fully comported with the DOJ/FTC Guidelines, the Defendant hospitals time and again sought and obtained RN wage-related information through direct contacts and surveys that fell short of the DOJ/FTC 'safety zone' criteria.").

20. European Commission, Guidelines on Horizontal Co-operation Agreements.

21. *Id.* at ¶ 61.

22. *Id.* at ¶¶ 75–76.

23. *Id.* at ¶ 77.

24. See the EU guidelines, which provide an example of forecasting employed by producers using a third-party independent market research company in a concentrated market (local production and sale of fresh bottled carrot juice) as an efficiency-enhancing vehicle to coordinate supply and demand. This is cited by the EU Commission as permissible forecasting activities. *Id.* at ¶100.

25. *Pacific Bell Tel. Co. v. Linkline Commc'ns, Inc.*, 555 U.S. 438, 450 (2009). See also U.S. Dep't of Justice and Federal Trade Comm'n, Horizontal Merger Guidelines (2010) § 1 ("When the Agencies investigate whether a merger may lead to a substantial lessening of non-price competition, they employ an approach analogous to that used to evaluate price competition.").

26. See, for example, Federal Trade Commissioner Julie Brill, The Intersection of Consumer Protection and Competition in the New World of Privacy, *Competition Policy International*, 7(1), 19 (Spring 2011) (noting potential antitrust concerns about trade associations setting privacy standards).

27. See generally *Allied Tube & Conduit Corp. v. Indian Head, Inc.*, 486 U.S. 492, 509-10 (1988) (where "an economically interested party exercises decision-making authority in formulating a product standard for a private association that comprises market participants," antitrust liability potentially exists).

28. 15 U.S.C. §§ 13 et seq. Price discrimination also implicates Section 2 of the Sherman Act, 15 U.S.C. § 2, Section 5 of the Federal Trade Commission Act, 15 U.S.C. § 45, as well as a host of state antitrust laws, but as a broad proposition Robinson-Patman Act jurisprudence generally guides the review of price discrimination under federal law and under many state laws.

29. 15 U.S.C. § 13(a). For a more detailed discussion, see generally, Douglas Kochelek, Data Mining and Antitrust, *Harvard Journal of Law and Technology*, 22(2), 515 (2009).

30. See generally *Ball Memorial Hospital v. Mutual Hospital Ins.*, 784 F.2d 1325, 1340 (7th Cir. 1986) (hospital services are not Robinson-Patman Act "commodities"); *Freeman v. Chicago Title & Trust Co.*, 505 F.2d 527, 530 (7th Cir. 1974) (title insurance); *Metro Communications Co. v. Ameritech Mobile Commc'ns, Inc.*, 984 F.2d 739, 745 (6th Cir. 1993) (cellular telephone service).

31. See, for example, *Wire Mesh Products, Inc. v. Wire Belting Assoc.*, 520 Supp. 1004, 1006 (E.D. Pa. 1981) (nonstandard and made-to-order wire belting material was not a commodity of "like grade and quality").

32. Such sellers, however, must be careful that their customized pricing does not otherwise violate state unfair trade practices or predatory pricing statutes.

33. See *Dynegy Marketing & Trade v. Multiut Corp.*, 648 F.3d 506, 522 (7th Cir. 2011).

34. See *Brooke Group Ltd. v. Brown & Williamson Tobacco Corp.*, 509 U.S. 209, 221 (1993).

9

The Impact of Big Data on Insureds, Insurance Coverage, and Insurers

Ethan D. Lenz and Morgan J. Tilleman

9.1 INTRODUCTION

This chapter discusses the impact of Big Data on the insurance industry, both from the perspective of businesses that purchase commercial insurance coverage and from the perspective of insurers. The first part of this chapter focuses on several topics that will have an impact on purchasers of insurance, including

- Risks posed by Big Data and the limitations of insurance coverage under traditional forms of insurance;
- New insurance products that have been, or are currently being, developed to protect businesses against risks posed by Big Data; and
- How these new insurance products work and how they may differ from more traditional insurance coverage forms, such as commercial general liability insurance.

Further in the chapter, we discuss topics that will specifically affect insurers, including

- How insurers are currently, and in the future will be, utilizing Big Data in their day-to-day operations; and
- The impact of insurance industry regulations on insurers' utilization of Big Data.

Big Data will pose challenges to both businesses that purchase insurance, in terms of appropriately structuring their insurance coverage, and to insurers, in terms of their regulatory compliance when utilizing Big Data.

9.2 THE RISKS OF BIG DATA

The use of Big Data and the application of analytics to Big Data by any business will give rise to legal risks. These risks might arise from any number of sources, such as the following:

- Professional liability risks associated with allegedly faulty analytics provided to clients;
- Claims arising from damaged or lost data belonging to clients and other third parties;
- Data privacy breaches caused by the wrongful disclosure of personally identifiable and other sensitive data; and
- Breach of laws or regulations seemingly unconnected to the analytics, such as antitrust laws (see Chapter 8, "The Antitrust Laws and Big Data"); discrimination and human resource laws (see Chapter 10, "Using Big Data to Manage Human Resources"); or breach of e-discovery obligations (see Chapter 11, "Big Data Discovery").

Furthermore, the costs associated with data privacy breaches and other claims associated with Big Data will likely pose a more significant risk to companies in many different lines of business than has been seen in the past. As the amount of data generated increases, so does the potential harm caused by a data breach and the potential for faulty or inadequate analysis of available data by data analytics service providers.[1] Experts now predict that the amount of data created every day will double every 40 months.[2]

Particularly in the realm of data breaches, the potential losses are very real; consumers and the plaintiff's bar are active in this space, and lawsuits frequently follow data breaches (see Chapters 4, "Privacy and Big Data," and 6, "Big Data and Risk Assessment"). In terms of insurance coverage, a recent draft empirical analysis of data breach litigation by Sasha Romanosky, David Hoffman, and Alessandro Acquisti[3] suggests two patterns that will make coverage critical for consumer-focused Big Data usage: First, the likelihood of a lawsuit increases as the number of consumer records breached increases; second, breaches of health care information are most likely to result in costly settlements (see also Chapter 5, "Federal and State Data Privacy Laws and Their Implications for the Creation and Use of Large Health Information Databases"). Significantly, in 2011, one report documented 855 separate data breaches that resulted in the loss of over 174 million data records.[4] Thus, the question of what insurance coverage is, or is not, available to cover losses arising from these myriad risks quickly becomes paramount for all businesses operating in a Big Data environment.

9.3 TRADITIONAL INSURANCE LIKELY CONTAINS SIGNIFICANT COVERAGE GAPS FOR THE RISKS POSED BY BIG DATA

Some of the risks discussed in the preceding section may be covered by existing insurance products, such as commercial general liability insurance, errors and omissions liability insurance, or directors' and officers' liability insurance. However, for the most part, such policies were not developed with an eye toward the risks presented by Big Data, and most have exclusions and other coverage limitations that may significantly limit the coverage available for exposures arising from Big Data. In particular, companies cannot assume that their current insurance programs will provide adequate coverage for data security breaches, other third-party liability exposures, or even first-party losses that might result from the utilization of Big Data. For example, a standard form commercial general liability insurance policy, which is the most common type of liability protection purchased by most businesses, likely provides limited, if any, protection for most liability arising from a data breach or other technology-related loss exposures. The reason for this is that commercial general liability policies, particularly those issued to companies that are involved in data-driven service industries, will now almost universally contain

> Insurance coverage for claims arising from the utilization and handling of Big Data is likely extremely limited under traditional forms of insurance such as commercial general liability or directors and officers liability insurance policies.

specific exclusions and other coverage limitations that preclude coverage for such claims. These exclusions and limitations include the following:

- provisions expressly excluding electronic data from the definition of covered property damage;
- a specific exclusion of coverage for most damages arising from the loss of use of, or damage to, electronic data;
- limitations of the definition of covered property damage to damage to tangible property only (data is typically considered intangible property)[5];
- exclusion of all "personal injury" liability coverage for businesses with significant technology-focused operations[6]; and
- endorsements that specifically exclude coverage for personal injury liability arising from any access to or disclosure of a person's or organization's confidential or personal information.

Furthermore, for publicly traded entities, the coverage for the company itself (i.e., when the company is named as a defendant in a claim) under a directors and officers liability insurance policy is typically limited to coverage for securities-related claims. Consequently, there is also likely little or no coverage for the company under its directors and officers coverage if it is sued by a customer or other third party for losses arising from handling their data.

Given the limitations under traditional insurance coverage forms, new products, primarily in the form of "cyber liability" coverage have become more prevalent in the insurance marketplace. As such, not only decision makers in all sorts of businesses will need to recognize the potential risks that accompany an increased use of data and analytics, but also risk managers and executives will need to understand how newer, and often more distinctive, forms of insurance coverage can facilitate the use of Big Data by offering protection for their business against its potential risks (along with the limitations of such coverage).

A cyber package policy will typically include coverage for both losses arising from third-party lawsuits and direct losses suffered by a company from interruption of its business and so on.

9.4 CYBER LIABILITY INSURANCE COVERAGE FOR THE RISKS POSED BY BIG DATA

Given the likely gaps in coverage under standard forms of commercial insurance, businesses that utilize Big Data as a part of their corporate strategy will typically need to explore the purchase of some type of "cyber liability," "technology errors and omissions," or "cyber package" insurance protection as part of their risk management program. Currently, there is no standardization among such policies, and the coverage can vary widely depending on the insurer that underwrites the coverage. However, most such policies are "menu" driven, allowing the insured to pick and choose among the types of coverage it desires to purchase, thereby allowing the insured to customize the protection to the particular risk profile of its business.

Some of the available options that will potentially provide coverage for not only liability but also a company's "first-party" financial losses[7] arising from security breaches and other technology-related risks posed by the utilization of Big Data include the following:

- **Professional Liability/Technology Errors and Omissions Liability Coverage.** This type of insurance covers liability arising from an insured's performance of professional services for third parties for a fee. It can be broadly tailored to provide coverage for a wide variety of business activities, from data aggregation and analysis services; to data storage services; to software as a service (SaaS) applications; and beyond. The key to such coverage is carefully considering the services a company provides and negotiating the "professional services" definition of the policy to ensure that it includes coverage for liability arising from all such services provided by a particular company. However, as discussed further in the chapter, it often only provides coverage for "damages" suffered by a third party and may not pick up certain costs that are often associated with privacy breaches.

- Technology errors and omissions coverage can be particularly valuable for insureds that are responsible for storing, aggregating, and analyzing or otherwise handling Big Data consisting of large volumes of third-party customer data. In this regard, it may cover liability arising from deficient security, and resulting loss of use, or misuse of consumer-related data if the insured's systems are breached and customer data is stolen or destroyed. Furthermore, it can potentially provide coverage for damages arising from faulty aggregation or analysis services that are provided to third parties. Again, such risk exposures are highly unlikely to be covered under standard form commercial general liability insurance policies, particularly for companies whose primary business involves the handling or analysis of large quantities of data.
- **Privacy Breach Cost Protection.** Many forms of technology errors and omissions liability coverage will cover damages that a third party suffers as a result of a privacy breach. However, the coverage may not extend to potentially significant costs associated with a privacy breach, such as notification of affected individuals or the costs of monitoring services that must be, or are voluntarily provided to, the affected individuals following a privacy breach event. For companies that handle large volumes of personal information, these costs can be crippling when there is a large-scale privacy breach. As such, privacy breach cost protection (or similar) coverage should often be purchased separately as part of a comprehensive cyber liability or cyber package insurance policy.
- **Privacy Law Breach Protection.** This coverage provides protection against regulatory investigations and actions that might arise from alleged breaches of privacy-related laws. Although such insurance likely will not cover the costs of actual fines or penalties incurred resulting from a regulatory action, as state and national governments become more proactive in enforcing privacy laws, the legal expenses associated with responding to investigations will necessarily increase. Therefore, privacy law breach protection-type coverage will likely become a more valuable part of a company's cyber insurance protection portfolio, particularly for those companies handling personally identifiable and other sensitive data.
- **Hardware and Software/Network Security Liability Protection.** Although technology errors and omissions coverage will provide protection against liability arising from services provided to others, it may

still leave a gap in coverage for companies if they are not directly providing services as part of their business activities. The best example might be a business that, as part of its data aggregation services, accesses nonclient third-party networks and inadvertently transmits a computer virus from its network to the nonclient networks. Although significant liability might arise from such an event, it may not be covered under the technology errors and omissions coverage because it did not directly arise from providing services to a third party for a fee. This potential gap can often be filled by purchasing separate hardware and software/network security liability protection.

- **Cyber-Related Business Interruption Coverage.** This is so-called first-party protection that provides insurance for direct losses suffered by a company as a result of an interruption in the availability, or degradation of availability, of its website, computer systems, or network. Particularly for companies with significant web presences, this can be a significant gap, as the coverage may be excluded from a standard form commercial property insurance policy and therefore must be separately purchased as part of a cyber package policy that provides both first-party and third-party protections.

- **Cyber Extortion Coverage.** One of the most recent protections added as an option to many cyber package policies is for losses arising from cyber extortion. This coverage is typically unavailable under any of the standard forms of commercial property insurance coverage and will provide coverage for ransoms and other amounts paid as a result of illegal threats to damage websites or computer and software or data systems by way of the threatened introduction of computer viruses/worms, logic bombs, Trojan horses, and so on.

9.5 CONSIDERATIONS IN THE PURCHASE OF CYBER INSURANCE PROTECTION

Cyber insurance protection is still in its relative infancy when placed in the context of traditional forms of insurance. The coverage forms have largely been developed since the mid-2000s, and insurers have only recently started to see significant increases in the overall volume of sales in the commercial insurance marketplace. Given this, both insurers and insureds continue to struggle with the exact scope of the protection that

Cyber liability insurance coverage typically differs from commercial general liability insurance coverage in at least two fundamental ways. First, attorneys' fees and other costs associated with defending a suit typically reduce the available limits of coverage. Second, a policy must be in place at the time a claim is made for there to be coverage.

insurers are willing to provide and insureds are willing to purchase. As noted, the policies are not standardized; therefore, most insurers are willing to negotiate the precise terms and conditions of their policy forms to "fit" the policies more precisely to the risk exposures faced by different insureds. Insureds should take advantage of this willingness of the insurers and attempt to carefully tailor the coverage to provide as broad protection as possible for their particular business. However, this can only be accomplished by investing the time and resources necessary to identify the risks posed by a company's Big Data strategy, which should follow a risk management paradigm, including the following:

- A comprehensive assessment of where, how, and when data flows throughout the organization and how Big Data is utilized (utilization of data flow mapping is helpful to most organizations when completing such an assessment; see Figure 4.1 on data flow mapping);
- An analysis of the potential loss exposures (e.g., exposure to claims for data breaches, lost or damaged customer data, provision of faulty data analytics, etc.) presented by this utilization of Big Data;
- The company's risk appetite for either retaining these risks or transferring/covering them via insurance; and
- Careful analysis and understanding of potentially available insurance coverage to ensure that appropriate forms of cyber insurance coverage are put in place and that gaps in protection are minimized.

9.6 ISSUES RELATED TO CYBER LIABILITY INSURANCE COVERAGE

In addition to ensuring that appropriate types of insurance are put in place to protect your business, you should keep in mind when purchasing cyber insurance protection that the coverage may respond differently, in at least two fundamental ways, than some of the more traditional forms of insurance coverage. First, under most commercial general liability insurance coverage, liability suit defense costs are usually covered in addition to the policy limits. However, under most technology errors and omissions insurance policies, defense costs reduce the limits of coverage available to pay any settlements or damage awards. Given that defense costs may mount quickly in a complicated technology-related lawsuit, this means that insurance buyers will need to carefully consider the appropriate limits for such coverage.

The second fundamental way cyber insurance may respond differently to a loss is in terms of which policy year of coverage will provide protection. In this regard, most traditional commercial general liability protection is written on what is called an "occurrence" basis. This means that the policy that was in effect when any bodily injury or property damage suffered by a third party occurs will provide coverage, no matter how far in the future any claim is made. In contrast, most technology errors and omissions insurance coverage is written on a "claims-made" basis, which means coverage is only available if a policy is still in place when a claim is actually made against the insured. Given this, even if a company ceases business operations, it may need to extend its insurance coverage into the future to ensure proper protection against liability and claims that relate to events that took place during the time it was actively operating in the technology or Big Data space. This is typically referred to as "tail" or "extended reporting period" coverage and is something a company will usually need to consider if it is acquired or if it otherwise ceases or wraps up its operations.

Cyber liability insurance protection will undoubtedly continue to rapidly evolve in the coming years. Given the limitations of traditional insurance coverage forms, it will likely become a cornerstone of insurance protection for companies with significant exposure to loss in the technology space and particularly companies that utilize Big Data in their day-to-day operations. Therefore, risk managers and other savvy insurance purchasers will be required to familiarize themselves with the forms of protection available and carefully undertake a cost-benefit analysis to determine if the coverage is a viable option to treat their Big-Data-related and other technology-related loss exposures.

The insurance regulators of all 50 states and the District of Columbia work together through the National Association of Insurance Commissioners (NAIC) to write model laws and regulations. With some modifications, these model laws are widely adopted by the states.

9.7 THE USE OF BIG DATA BY INSURERS

Insurance companies' increasing use of data analytics and the development of larger and more sophisticated datasets have the potential to dramatically change the marketing, underwriting, and service capabilities of insurance companies; however, insurance regulation poses at least two potential issues for insurance companies seeking to further leverage data analytics using Big Data. Unlike many other industries, insurance is exempted from many federal regulations and is instead subject to state-by-state regulation.[8]

Three model laws will likely have the greatest impact on the growth and development of insurance company use of data analytics: the NAIC Model Privacy of Consumer Financial and Health Information Regulation (the Privacy Regulation), the NAIC Insurance Information and Privacy Protection Model Act (the Privacy Act), and the NAIC Model Unfair Trade Practices Act (the Trade Practices Act).

9.8 UNDERWRITING, DISCOUNTS, AND THE TRADE PRACTICES ACT

Insurers have always been able to use information about applicants to engage in underwriting; indeed, this is one of the central functions of an insurance company. From application forms to property inspections and audits, insurers seek to obtain the best possible picture of their insureds and the risks their insureds face in order to adequately price insurance coverage while competing for business in the highly competitive market. Big Data can be a powerful tool to improve underwriting; witness the efforts taken by automobile insurers to secure more data about individual drivers through programs like Progressive's "Snapshot" device.[9] Even though better underwriting benefits both consumers (who can see premium reductions) and insurers (who can better predict their future losses and thereby improve underwriting results), state laws, including the Trade Practices Act, currently restrict the ability of insurers to make use of granular information about particular insureds. The Trade Practices Act prohibits certain "unfair discrimination" in insurance pricing; although this concept is not explicitly defined in the Trade Practices Act, both general understanding in the insurance world and the limited number of published cases available define impermissible or unfair discrimination as discrimination that is not actuarially justified.[10]

For example, Texas law contains an explicit exemption from the prohibition on discriminatory pricing for rates that vary based on actuarial analysis. Texas Insurance Code § 544.053 (a) states: "A person does not violate Section 544.052 [which prohibits discriminatory pricing] if the refusal to insure or to continue to insure, the limiting of the amount, extent, or kind of coverage, or the charging of an individual a rate that is different from the rate charged another individual for the same coverage is based on sound actuarial principles." In other states, this principle is established by case law. Take Maryland, where the state supreme court has held that unfair (and thus prohibited) discrimination "means discrimination among insureds of the same class based upon something other than actuarial risk."[11] As a general principle, it is fair to say that the act allows pricing based on actuarial principles. Accordingly, insurance may be priced or underwritten based on factors that can be demonstrated through actuarial analysis to have an actuarially significant impact on the relevant risk. In all cases, whether personal lines automobile or large commercial property and liability or workers' compensation, insurers will need to use analytics in actuarially sound ways to avoid violating the Trade Practices Act.

Large insurers that have already started to amass data about their insureds (Progressive, State Farm, and Allstate each have car-interface devices in the market, for example) will no doubt be able to demonstrate the actuarial value of this information in many cases. Auto insurers have already been able to identify risk profiles using their car-interface devices. In 2012, the *New York Times* reported: "Allstate says the lowest-risk time for accidents is 5 a.m. to 11 p.m. on weekends, with the highest risk from 11 p.m. to 4 a.m. on weekdays and 11 p.m. to 5 a.m. on weekends."[12] Consequently, drivers who drive during high-risk hours may face higher rates (or simply miss out on discounts). This information, and other information that insurers already know, or will learn in the future, does not appear immediately after implementing a data-driven underwriting process; insurers must first invest time, energy, and substantial financial resources in collecting and connecting the data that can support robust actuarial analysis and the resulting underwriting differentiation. Thus far, these data-driven underwriting tools have been widely employed by some of the largest insurers; State Farm, Allstate, and Progressive are titans of the insurance world with plenty of resources to invest in such tools. The development of a Snapshot-like tool at smaller automobile and other insurers may prove to be a greater challenge given the number of insureds and the smaller scale of resources. Thus, the ability to develop and deploy data collection devices and conduct analytics, even of information generated by a single source (like the car-interface device), may provide a competitive pricing advantage to large, resource-rich insurers.

Although automobile insurance is perhaps the type of coverage for which data-driven pricing is most visible, the combination of first- and third-party data seems likely to become an increasing part of the insurance industry's practices in other lines of coverage as well. The use of third-party data raises significant compliance risks with respect to the Privacy Act and Privacy Regulation, as we explain further in this chapter. Indeed, large and sophisticated consultancies are marketing their Big Data services to insurers across a broad spectrum of lines. For example, IBM advertises its ability to align data sources and underwriting for all types of insurers,[13] while Milliman touts its ability to achieve Big Data insights for small insurers.[14] Similarly, Sam Medina of Tata Consultancy Services Limited recently told *Business Insurance*: "There is not a single commercial lines carrier that we deal with that does not have Big Data on their agenda."[15]

9.9 THE PRIVACY ACT

The Privacy Act's purpose is to establish standards for the collection, use, and disclosure of consumer information in connection with insurance transactions.[16] Clearly, it will have an impact on the use of Big Data in insurance underwriting and marketing. Insurers have three primary obligations under the Privacy Act that will apply to the data underlying Big Data:

(1) the obligation to permit consumers access to information about themselves; (2) the obligation to correct, amend, or delete inaccurate personal information about consumers; and (3) the obligation to disclose data-driven adverse underwriting decisions. Because of the substantially larger amount of data now being collected, connected, and used, the compliance process will be more involved and the potential regulatory risks larger for insurers who use Big Data in their underwriting and pricing decisions.

9.10 ACCESS TO PERSONAL INFORMATION

Section 8 of the Privacy Act obligates insurers, insurance agents, and insurance support organizations to provide individuals with access to personal information that is held by such entities on written request. The Privacy Act has a broad definition of personal information; it includes "any individual identifiable information gathered in connection with an insurance transaction from which judgments can be made about an individual's character, habits, avocations, finances, occupation, general reputation, credit, health or any other personal characteristics." Collecting and understanding this type of information is a primary purpose for the use of Big Data by insurance companies; accordingly, a large portion, if not all, of the underlying data will be subject to disclosure to consumers pursuant to the Privacy Act, as discussed in the following material. This poses several potential problems for insurers.

Unlike traditional credit reports and other datasets used in underwriting, Big Data databases are not generally consumer friendly; that is, their contents are not readily accessible and understandable to laypersons. The disclosure of such information, even about a limited number of insureds, could confuse or anger customers who may not have any understanding of what Big Data is or how it is actually used by insurers. Second, such disclosure could reveal an insurance company's Big Data strategy by showing what sorts of information a particular company felt were important enough to utilize in its underwriting process. Third, the sheer magnitude of Big Data databases makes the required disclosure more challenging. For example, providing access to a summary credit report is relatively simple, but giving consumers access to their Big Data records will be substantially more burdensome because of the sheer quantity of data in question. Because the Privacy Act does not distinguish between first- and third-party data, insurers will potentially need to provide access to both types of data for consumers who make Privacy Act requests. As insurers increase the amount of data they utilize in making underwriting and coverage decisions, the cost of compliance with Section 8 of the Privacy Act will increase rapidly as well. Insurers will need to be aware of the potential costs imposed by the disclosure obligation and factor the cost and inconvenience of potential future disclosures into decisions that are made as analytics are deployed across their business.

9.11 CORRECTION OF PERSONAL INFORMATION

Like credit agencies, insurance companies that maintain consumer databases are obligated to respond to requests for correction regarding recorded personal information. Section 9 of the Privacy Act gives insurers 30 business days to respond to written requests for changes, corrections, and deletions of specific personal information from consumers, either by correcting recorded information or providing written notification, and reasons for a refusal to do so. As databases grow, the potential volume of challenges grows as well; consumers will have a much larger amount of data to challenge, which will require insurers to dedicate more human and information technology resources to evaluating and responding to consumer challenges to stored or connected personal information. This is a second collateral impact of expanding the use of Big Data that will be important for insurers to consider in implementing data-driven marketing and underwriting. Insurers must therefore ensure that stored and connected personal information is subject to correction pursuant to the Privacy Act, even information that remains in the possession of third-party providers at all times.

9.12 DISCLOSURE OF THE BASIS
FOR ADVERSE UNDERWRITING DECISIONS

Section 10 of the Privacy Act requires that insurers provide consumers with specific written explanations of adverse underwriting decisions. On consumer request, the insurer must also furnish specific items of personal information that underlie such adverse underwriting decisions. For underwriting decisions based on Big Data and its analytics, this disclosure will be complicated by the very nature of dynamic analysis and Big Data. There may no longer be one or even a handful of data points that cause an adverse decision; instead, there will be a whole universe of data points that, taken together, inform underwriting decisions. In this sense, the increasing use of Big Data may fundamentally alter the nature of disclosure for adverse underwriting decisions. Although such a notice today might simply state that a consumer's driving record contains too many traffic violations and the excess of violations caused the adverse underwriting decision, a disclosure in the world of Big Data may need to provide the consumer with an explanation of the analytics process as well as the data points that underlie its analysis. This will be an area of the law to watch closely: The recently released report on insurance regulatory modernization completed by the Federal Insurance Office suggests that data-driven underwriting should be even more thoroughly regulated, with the scope of insurers' use of personal information in underwriting limited by law and regulation.[17] Nevertheless, the practical nature of disclosure is likely to change because of the change in the nature of data underlying insurance underwriting.

Disclosure of personal data, correction of challenged personal data, and disclosure of the bases for adverse underwriting decisions are not new obligations for insurers. The sheer magnitude of personal data that may be used in Big Data analytics makes this task a compliance concern in ways that insurers' existing uses of personal information do not, however. Compliance professionals as well as data specialists will need to be mindful of the challenges posed by insurers' use of Big Data as insurers embark on more complicated and more numerous data analytics projects. Although compliance will be an ongoing challenge, insurers should consider the following general principles as they build analytic platforms and deploy Big Data in their marketing and underwriting:

- Commercial analytics solutions are likely not set up for insurance law compliance out of the box.
- Compliance can no longer be an after-the-fact response handled solely by compliance professionals.
- Analytic platforms and processes must take into account the legal obligations imposed by state insurance regulations. For example, insurers must be able to identify the third-party information actually utilized in their Big Data analyses with respect to specific consumer months, or even years, after such analysis occurred.

- Legal and compliance professionals at insurance companies must closely monitor developments at the state and federal levels to maintain compliance on a going-forward basis.

9.13 THIRD-PARTY DATA AND THE PRIVACY ACT

The disclosure obligations imposed by the Privacy Act described previously do not differentiate between personal information collected directly by the insurer (on an application or using an auto-interface device, for example) and third-party information. This has always been true, and insurers regularly use credit reports, driving histories, and other third-party sources of information to evaluate and underwrite potential risks. However, the governments and credit reporting organizations that prepare these traditional types of third-party data are subject to public disclosure requirements in their business as well; that is not necessarily the case for other types of third-party data vendors who may be sources of data used in Big Data analytics. However, should third-party data be used by insurers to perform data-driven underwriting, the insurers would be obligated to disclose such third-party data pursuant to the provisions of Sections 8 and 10 of the Privacy Act. Insurers will need to secure contractual rights to reveal such information when required under the Privacy Act and similar laws if third-party data is to be utilized in underwriting or sales activities. While this is not a new type of obligation for insurers, who already receive information from Insurance Services Office Incorporated (ISO), MIB Group, Inc., and other third-party data providers, next-generation data providers not focused on the insurance industry may need to be educated by insurance company clients to ensure that these compliance obligations are provided for by contract and achieved by third-party providers.

9.14 THE PRIVACY REGULATION

The Privacy Regulation requires insurance companies to provide notice of their information privacy practices to their customers and imposes certain restrictions and conditions on the use of customers' personal information by insurance companies, their affiliates, and third parties. The Privacy

Regulation has many parallels with the portions of the Gramm-Leach-Bliley ("GLB") Act,[18] which applies to financial institutions. Unlike other financial institutions, insurers are also subject to state privacy laws specifically governing the insurance industry. Among those laws are many based on the Privacy Regulation. There are two provisions in the Privacy Regulation that potentially will have an impact on data analytics at insurance companies. These provisions are (1) the requirement that consumers be allowed to opt out of information sharing with nonaffiliated third parties and (2) prohibition of discrimination against consumers who have opted out of information sharing.

To the extent that an insurer wants to participate fully in the world of Big Data, it may desire not only to receive third-party information but also to sell or otherwise share its own first-party data with other third parties. Much like banks and other noninsurance financial institutions must do under the GLB Act, insurers are obligated by Section 12 of the Privacy Regulation to give consumers a privacy notice and the chance to opt out of information sharing with third parties. If an insurer desires to share its own data with others, it will need to update its privacy notices and give consumers the chance to opt out of that data sharing. Should a consumer opt out of disclosure of information to third parties, Section 24 of the Privacy Regulation prohibits any discrimination or other actions taken in response.

9.15 CONCLUSION

The utilization of Big Data and the implementation of Big-Data-related business strategies will pose myriad challenges for both purchasers of commercial insurance coverage and all insurers. Insurance purchasers will need to:

- Carefully assess the new loss exposures created by the utilization of Big Data and implementation of Big Data business strategies;
- Understand the coverage and limitations under their traditional insurance programs; and
- Undertake a carefully planned risk management analysis to ensure that any cyber package or similar insurance policies they intend to utilize to cover their Big Data exposures are comprehensive enough to accomplish that goal.

With respect to insurers, the most significant challenges arising from the utilization of Big Data and Big-Data-driven strategies will be:

- The determination of the Big Data strategies that can be justified in their marketing, underwriting, and service operations; and
- Understanding and adhering to the regulatory challenges and requirements that will arise from their existing obligations to policyholders.

Although the challenges faced by both insurance purchasers and insurers are not insignificant by any means, through careful assessment and implementation of appropriate strategies, as discussed in this chapter, both will be well on their way to navigating these challenges and appropriately protecting their businesses.

NOTES

1. For example, if a service provider is retained to gather data and create an algorithm to analyze that data, it might be exposed to liability for failure to gather a sufficient amount of relevant data, missing relevant data points, or failing to create an algorithm that appropriately analyzes the data based on its clients' needs.
2. Andrew McAfee and Erik Brynjolfsson. Big Data: The Management Revolution. *Harvard Business Review* (October 2012).
3. Sasha Romanosky, David Hoffman, and Allesandro Acquisti. Empirical Analysis of Data Breach Litigation. Draft available at http://ssrn.com/abstract=1986461.
4. Verizon RISK Team. 2012 Data Breach Investigations Report. 2012. Available at http://www.verizonbusiness.com/resources/reports/rp_data-breach-investigations-report-2012_en_xg.pdf.
5. While court decisions are not universal on the subject, the majority rule in most US jurisdictions appears to lean toward finding that data is intangible property, and therefore damage resulting from lost or damaged data falls outside the coverage of a policy that limits the definition of covered "property damage" to tangible property.
6. "Personal injury" liability coverage under the standard form commercial general liability insurance policy typically includes coverage for publication of material that violates a person's right of privacy, and insureds have previously utilized this definition to argue for coverage for data breach liability claims.
7. In insurance terms, liability insurance typically covers defense costs and judgments or settlements arising from third-party claims against a person or business. On the other hand, "first-party" coverage refers to insurance for a business for direct losses the business suffers to property that it owns (e.g., costs associated with re-creating data that the business owns).
8. The McCarran-Ferguson Act, 15 U.S.C. §§ 1011-1015.
9. The Snapshot device is a small automotive interface device that attaches directly to the On-Board Diagnostics (OBD-II) port in an automobile. It collects and transmits

to Progressive information about the driving behavior of a customer, including incidences of hard braking and the number of miles driven each day.

10. Actuarial analysis is the application of statistical methods to the evaluation of the financial consequences of risk. Actuaries evaluate the likelihood of uncertain future events and the potential insurance costs of such events according to principles set forth in Actuarial Standards of Practice adopted by the Actuarial Standards Board. See http://www.actuarialstandardsboard.org/asops.asp. Because of the centrality of actuarial analysis to the operation of insurance companies, state regulators frequently defer to such analyses when evaluating the underwriting and pricing activities of insurers.

11. *Insurance Comm'r for the State v. Engelman*, 345 Md. 402 (1997).

12. Randall Stross. So You're a Good Driver? Let's Go to the Monitor. *The New York Times*, November 24, 2012. Available at http://www.nytimes.com/2012/11/25/business/seeking-cheaper-insurance-drivers-accept-monitoring-devices.html?_r=0.

13. See http://www-935.ibm.com/services/us/gbs/thoughtleadership/big-data-insurance/.

14. See http://www.milliman.com/insight/2013/Why-big-data-is-a-big-deal/.

15. Bill Kenealy. Commercial Insurers Embrace Big Data. *Business Insurance*, December 16, 2013, at 4.

16. While the Gramm-Leach-Bliley Act (GLBA) (Financial Services Modernization Act of 1999, Pub.L. 106-102, 113 Stat. 1338) generally governs the privacy practices of financial institutions, GLBA does not preempt state laws governing insurers' privacy practices so long as such laws are at least equivalent to GLBA (15 U.S.C. § 6807). State laws based on the Privacy Act are equivalent to GLBA, although some states have enacted more restrictive privacy laws with respect to insurance. For thorough discussion of GLBA, see Chapter 2, "Overview of Information Security and Compliance: Seeing the Forest for the Trees."

17. Federal Insurance Office. *How to Modernize and Improve the System of Insurance Regulation in the United States.* U.S. Department of the Treasury, December 2013, at pp. 56–57.

18. Financial Services Modernization Act of 1999 (Pub.L. 106-102, 113 Stat. 1338).

10

Using Big Data to Manage Human Resources

Mark J. Neuberger

10.1 INTRODUCTION

The human resource function of any organization is especially well positioned to benefit from the business decision-making insights offered by Big Data. The ability to gain insight into the future and past behavior of employees is a key component to marshaling the power of people to better achieve desired organizational outcomes. This chapter

- Discusses the value of Big Data to enhance the human resource function of any organization;
- Reviews various case studies demonstrating how Big Data is already helping some organizations manage their human resources with greater efficiency; and
- Explains how certain legal concepts with an impact on human resource activities can create risks in connection with the use of Big Data.

Often, the human resource function in an organization is viewed as the enforcer of rules and regulations—something like an internal police force. In such organizations, the prevailing perception is that human resources are there to tell people what the rules are and to enforce them. Sometimes, human resources are seen as a proxy social worker/employee advocate. Neither of these views fairly recognizes the value an effective human resource function can deliver to the enterprise. When optimized, a human resource function has the characteristics described by Sharlyn Lauby, a human resource consultant on her Human Resource Bartender blog: "The value of human resources is that they are the great equalizer. Human Resource is the creator of balance between the interests of management and the interests of employees. When a proper balance is achieved, companies get the best performance from their employees. And employees are engaged with their work. It's a win for everyone involved."[1] This value can be materially enhanced in any organization through the use of Big Data by enabling human resource managers to assist managers to make informed decisions regarding personnel onboarding, engagement, discipline, and termination and thereby support specific organizational goals, like increasing profitability and improving talent management and retention.

Historically, human resource managers have spent large amounts of time reporting on past events, including calculating the turnover of new hires, calculating the absenteeism rate of employees, and reporting how much money has been spent on compensation and benefits. Big Data represents a tremendous opportunity to shift the focus of human resource departments by leveraging data about employees to improve the efficiency and efficacy of an organization. The use of predictive analytics to help make better decisions regarding who to hire, who to promote, who to reassign or terminate, and how to compensate to motivate increased employee performance are just some of the benefits that can come from the use of Big Data.

As discussed in the examples that follow, often the use of Big Data will debunk conventional myths about the management of people in organizations. For example, in the quest to drive employee performance ever higher, organizations spend significant time and effort attempting to manage the balance between paying the least amount of money to achieve the greatest amount of performance. However, research studies going back decades have consistently proven that money frequently is clearly not one of the top factors motivating employees.[2] In *Drive*,[3] a 2009 book that examines multiple social experiments, the author demonstrates that intrinsic motivators like the internal desire to do good work, the ability to advance one's career, and recognition by supervisors and peers are far greater motivators than money and benefits. Big Data represents a way to identify those intrinsic motivators within a workforce and to allow managers to better reward and motivate employees.

Many forms of analytical projects that have traditionally been performed by human resource managers can be managed using fairly basic databases. However, Big Data represents the opportunity to take data analysis to the next level; instead of reporting on what has already transpired, predictive analytics can help paint the picture of a likely future. However, those seeking to use Big Data analytics in the human resource function of their organizations must be sensitive to the likely perception that the organization is replacing sound human judgment from managers with "statistics" created by "number crunchers." This perception should not likely prevail, however, because to optimize the value of Big Data, organizations will achieve a balance between the data scientists understanding the limits of their analysis and human resource managers understanding that the data is there to support, not supplant, the day-to-day decisions that they must make. The processes must also allow individual managers to apply their experience and judgment while debunking myths and prejudices so that decisions are made with empirical evidence informed by human judgment. When numerically based analytics are harmonized with experiential decision making, the introduction of Big Data into human resource processes will be optimized and more readily accepted.

10.2 USING BIG DATA TO MANAGE PEOPLE

If you are considering how to use Big Data to manage your people resources, there are already many excellent examples from leading companies that are instructive. Several summaries of how leading organizations have used Big Data in their human resource activities are presented in this section. These examples nicely illustrate opportunities that are available to most organizations.

10.2.1 Absenteeism and Scheduling

Google learned that during the annual flu season, people start searching the web for information on flu symptoms and flu remedies. Google describes the process they use as follows:

> We have found a close relationship between how many people search for flu-related topics and how many people actually have flu symptoms. Of course, not every person who searches for "flu" is actually sick, but a pattern emerges when all the flu-related search queries are added together. We compared our query counts with traditional flu surveillance systems and found that many search queries tend to be popular exactly when flu season is happening. By counting how often we see these search queries, we can estimate how much flu is circulating in different countries and regions around the world.[4]

Google Flu Trends is not perfect; during the 2013 flu season, it over-estimated the occurrence of flu in the United States by over 25%.[5] However, when real-time estimates from Google Flu Trends and data from the Centers for Disease Control and Prevention (CDC) surveillance are combined, they reliably predicted the timing of the 2012–2013 influenza season up to 9 weeks in advance of its peak.[6] The process will continue to be refined by Google and others. However, the potential for managers to use this type of insight can help businesses prepare for flu and other pandemics by anticipating the outbreak, allowing management to take preventive measures, including lining up contingent workers or advancing production ahead of an impending onslaught of employee absenteeism.

10.2.2 Identifying Attributes of Success for Various Roles

In its continual search to look for workers to staff its call centers, Xerox would historically focus its search for job applicants by looking for people who had previous call center experience. After running a Big Data analysis on hiring and turnover, Xerox discovered that the prior job experience of its candidates was not a strong indicator of success in the role. It learned that what made a successful call center employee was a certain personality type. Searching for those who were inquisitive and creative, the traits revealed through their data analysis, Xerox was able to reduce its call center attrition by 20%.[7] Xerox further discovered that formal education was similarly irrelevant. Like most other employers, Xerox's selection process historically focused on a candidate's education and experience as revealed in an application form and resume. After undergoing a Big Data analysis, the focus of the selection process was changed to personality tests and data analysis.

The use of Big Data in hiring, especially in technology-related jobs, is causing more employers to look at candidates who, using conventional wisdom, they would have never otherwise considered. Increasingly, employers are looking at people who did not attend or graduate from college because their analytics revealed no benefit whatsoever to hiring people with college degrees. Alternatively, Big Data has shown employers there are factors that function as far better predictors of future job performance that allows for hiring people who do not fill the traditional mold of those with college-related coursework.[8]

10.2.3 Leading Change

ConAgra Foods became concerned when it realized that over 50% of its current employees would be eligible to retire in the next ten years. This triggered a need to ensure hiring people with the right skills to replace those departing workers. Knowing the extent of the organizational change that was coming, it was of primary importance to search for people who could easily adapt to job change. Using Big Data analytics, ConAgra learned that its conventional assumption that younger people were more adept at learning new tasks was false. Rather, ConAgra discovered that the ability to easily learn new tasks is basically an interpersonal skill that can be present at any age.[9] By using Big Data, ConAgra was also able to predict which employees were more likely to quit. By analyzing data in the portions of the company that had significantly higher turnover, ConAgra was able to identify factors that cause people to leave. ConAgra found that lack of recognition and nonmonetary rewards drove people away more than any concerns over their pay and benefits.

The lesson to be learned from the Xerox and ConAgra Foods examples is that conventional myths regarding who best to hire and who best to invest in by way of training and promotions are being challenged by data. Businesses that can isolate what is truly relevant to ensuring better performance on the job are learning that traditional assumptions of the skills that make for an optimal new hire may not only be mistaken but also may be obstacles to hiring and retaining an engaged and more productive workforce.

10.2.4 Managing Employee Fraud

Another example of the successful application of Big Data is in the food service industry, for which analytical software is being used to cut down on employee fraud. By some estimates, employee fraud costs the US economy as much as $200 billion a year. In the restaurant industry, where profit margins are especially thin, anything that will eliminate fraud can have immediate bottom-line benefits for the business. Software programs have been developed that alert restaurants to billing irregularity trends, with one of the red flags for fraud being an unusual number of partially completed or voided checks. Additional red flags are a high occurrence of lower-priced menu items like beverages, all of which are statistical indications that an employee may be pocketing some of the money from such transactions. Tracking these trends reveals what has been commonly referred to as the "wagon wheel scam": Waiters sell numerous sodas throughout a shift but keep the money for most of those transactions. They ring up a soda for one customer but leave the check open and temporarily transfer the charge to another patron. By studying keystrokes and trends in the checks being rung up through the system, restaurants can spot these scams and shut down the theft.[10]

These examples of how some companies use Big Data in the human resource function demonstrate that using Big Data may call into question conventional assumptions about how to manage people. There may be better and different ways to achieve desired organizational outcomes than those employed today.

10.3 REGULATING THE USE OF BIG DATA IN HUMAN RESOURCE MANAGEMENT

A number of federal laws that regulate the employment process may have an impact on the use of Big Data when applied to human resource management. Although due consideration must be given to the legal framework, none of these laws in and of themselves prevents the use of Big Data. Managers contemplating using Big Data to assist in employment decision making need to be wary of potential legal limitations on the use of the insights from their searches and structure their analysis and decisions accordingly.

10.4 ANTIDISCRIMINATION UNDER TITLE VII

Title VII of the Civil Rights Act of 1964 is the granddaddy of antidiscrimination legislation.[11] It prohibits all forms of employment discrimination on the basis of race, color, religion, national origin, and sex. Under Title VII, two theories of discrimination have evolved through court decisions: disparate treatment and disparate or adverse impact. The first, disparate treatment, is much easier to understand. Treating someone differently because of their race, color, or national origin is illegal. We all know refusing to hire anyone simply because the person is a member of one of these protected groups is illegal. Disparate impact, on the other hand, presents a more nuanced theory of discrimination. It holds that seemingly neutral employment practices may be illegal if they have a disproportionate, or more adverse, impact on members of a protected group. This theory prohibits an employer from using a facially neutral employment practice that has an unjustified adverse impact on the members of the protected category.[12] Whenever a facially neutral policy is shown to have such a disparate impact on members of a legally protected group, an employer can defend its actions by proving that the policy is reasonably and rationally related to the job for which it is being required.

A classic example in which the disparate impact theory has been used to find illegal discrimination is in height requirements. Before the passage of Title VII, it was common for police departments to impose a specific minimum height requirement as a condition for admission to the police academy. On its face, the policy treats everyone the same. However, statistically women, and perhaps members of certain minority groups, are less likely to meet the standard. They will therefore be screened out at much higher rates, or disparately impacted. That makes for a prima facie case of illegal discrimination. However, to the extent the employer can demonstrate a rational basis for why people of that height are more likely to be better-performing police officers, they can rebut the prima facie case. Most police departments that used such standards could not make such a showing, and today, such requirements are no longer used.

One area in which use of Big Data could run up against the disparate impact theory of discrimination is through increased use of tests in making employment-related decisions. Any time an employer develops a selection device like a test, the device being used should be properly assessed by professionals trained in the use of human measurement devices. To withstand the inevitable legal challenge to the use of tests, employers must be prepared to produce to either plaintiff's counsel or a prosecuting governmental agency like the EEOC (Equal Employment Opportunity Commission) the necessary statistical analysis. At a minimum, that analysis must include a showing that the manner and method of testing in each particular organization can be statistically shown to be both reliable (meaning it tests the same thing each time it is used) and a valid predictor. Typically, the development of such statistical analysis will require engaging a professional psychometrician. As seen in some of the case studies presented, employers who use Big Data may increasingly seek to make decisions based on such factors as identifiable personality traits. This may drive employers to the use of tests and other selection devices to isolate candidates with the desired traits. Often, such tests have demonstrated disparate impact. In fact, in the *Griggs* case cited previously in this section (see Note 12), the Duke Power Company was found to have historically segregated Black employees into the lowest classification of jobs. After the passage of Title VII, the company eliminated overt segregation but imposed passing an IQ test as a prerequisite for moving to a higher-classified job. Statistically, Black employees in North Carolina in the 1960s did not perform as well on such tests and therefore were limited in their career progression. When they were sued, the companies could not demonstrate that increased IQ was a successful predictor of future job performance for the jobs in the power plant in question. As a result, the use of these tests was found to violate Title VII.

The lesson here is not that all tests are discriminatory. Rather, if an employer wants to use tests, the employer must do so properly (see Table 10.1). To do that, employers must conform their practices to a comprehensive set of regulations known as the Uniform Guidelines on Employee Selection Procedures.[13] In 1978, four federal agencies, including the EEOC and the US Department of Labor, issued this joint regulation. The guidelines apply to tests and other selection procedures used as the basis for any type of employment decision, including hiring, promotion, demotion, retention, and compensation. The guidelines establish how an employer, using a selection device like testing, must demonstrate that (1) the test adopted is both reliable and consistent among the parties to

TABLE 10.1

Dos and Don'ts of Preemployment Testing

Dos	Don'ts
Undertake a proper job analysis to identify criteria that you can statistically demonstrate predict future job success	Use conventional assumptions about what you think are the critical indicators of successful performance
Use professionally developed tests that measure criteria identified in job analysis	Use a homemade test you think will work and will save time and money
Analyze the selected test's adverse impact on legally protected groups, and if it does impact adversely, explore alternatives	Assume that because the test is "objective" you can defend its use in the face of adverse impact on legally protected groups
Develop methods to accommodate disabled test takers	Treat everyone the same, all the time
Train those who will administer the tests as well as those who will make placement decisions using test results; make sure everyone understands the legal framework of testing	Just follow the instructions and do not look back

whom it is being administered, and (2) it is, in fact, a valid predictor of the performance it intends to assess. For example, the SAT and ACT college admission tests have been consistently validated to predict future performance in one thing and one thing only: one's performance as a first-year college student. Therefore, an employer using the SAT or ACT to hire or promote individuals within an organization, absent some additional study and analysis by trained testing experts, would be deemed an invalid use and therefore an improper defense against a showing of adverse impact.

Testing for predictive indicators can be an extremely valuable tool in selecting and retaining engaged employees. As seen from some of the examples presented, employers can perform analytical research to isolate the skills criteria that are predictive indicators for success in their particular organization. In such circumstances, they then can test for those skills, be it among candidate pools or among their current workforce. However, use of criteria that cannot be statistically validated to support the job-related criteria, and the use of tests that have not been scientifically proven to be reliable measurements of how the test measures criteria which predict job performance will likely run afoul of the Uniform Guidelines. The takeaway for employers contemplating the use of tests to help make decisions in any aspect of the employment process is that if they are going to do it, they need to do it right. That requires consulting with testing and legal experts and not pulling tests off the shelf and doing what may intuitively make sense. After all, as we have seen, so much about the use of Big Data involves debunking myths and moving beyond conventional wisdom.

10.5 THE GENETIC INFORMATION AND NONDISCRIMINATION ACT OF 2007

The Genetic Information and Nondiscrimination Act of 2007 (GINA)[14] is also administered by the EEOC. Under GINA, it is illegal for employers to discriminate against either employees or applicants because of their genetic information. GINA also prohibits employers from requesting, requiring, or purchasing genetic information about their employees. Under GINA, genetic information is defined in very broad terms and includes genetic testing not only of the individual but also of their family members. This includes information about potential diseases or disorders the employee or their family members may experience. Family medical history is also included in the law's definition of information because, historically, it has been used to determine whether an employee has an increased risk of disease, disorder, or condition in the future. GINA prohibits discrimination based on the use of genetic information in any aspect of employment and further prohibits employers from harassing or retaliating against an individual because the individual has objected to improper use of their genetic information. Thus, the accumulation of anything that constitutes genetic information to predict whether an employee may be more susceptible to disease, or future performance issues because of their genetic makeup, will run afoul of GINA.

As employers struggle to contain the cost of providing medical insurance to their employees and try to maintain the health of an aging workforce, there has been an explosion of employee wellness programs. A wellness program is defined in section 2705(j)(1)(A) of the Public Health Service Act[15] as any program offered by an employer designed to promote health or prevent disease. Certain types of wellness programs offered through employment-based group health plan coverage must now meet standards under the Affordable Care Act.[16] There is a veritable potpourri of workplace wellness programs that run the gamut from benefits aimed to promote health-related behaviors such as free or discounted gym memberships, diet education or smoking cessation programs, to early identification and better management of chronic diseases like diabetes or epilepsy. To be effective, wellness programs typically include data collection to preidentify employee health risks, which can then be used to craft interventions to reduce those risks.

When used in the employee wellness area, Big Data may bump up against the variety of privacy concerns and laws described elsewhere in this book as well as GINA. GINA, however, provides a safe harbor for employers: Where health or genetic services are

> offered by the employer ... as part of a wellness program; the employee provides prior, knowing, voluntary, and written authorization; only the employee (or family member if the family member is receiving genetic services) and the licensed health care professional or board certified genetic counselor involved in providing such services receive individually identifiable information concerning the results of such services; and any individually identifiable genetic information provided is ... not [to] be disclosed to the employer except in aggregate terms that do not disclose the identity of specific employees.[17]

Thus, like the other employment-related laws discussed thus far, GINA does not preclude employers from using Big Data to measure and assess employee health, but it is a restriction that must be carefully navigated. Carefully analyze the various "safe harbors" contained in GINA and use them. Increasingly popular employee wellness programs are a common area where employers could run afoul of GINA. However, by ensuring the employer only sees aggregated and deidentified data about the health of its employees, the employees' rights under GINA can be preserved.

10.6 NATIONAL LABOR RELATIONS ACT

Contrary to conventional wisdom, the National Labor Relations Act (NLRA) does not simply apply to employers who have unions. In fact, the NLRA's legal protection extends to all the employees of those employers covered by it, which are those private-sector employers engaged in interstate commerce, excluding railroads and airlines. The NLRA allows all employees, whether or not they are represented by a union, to engage in what is known as "protected concerted activity." Protected concerted activity is generally defined as two or more employees taking action over some aspect of their hours worked, wages, compensation, and other terms and conditions of employment. Under the law, even a single employee may engage in activities that are deemed "concerted" under the NLRA.

Those employees who discuss their pay and benefits or complain about their working conditions will in most cases be protected by the NLRA. In addition to providing employees with certain rights, the NLRA restricts employers from engaging in certain activities that are deemed to be *unfair labor practices* (ULPs). Employers commit an ULP whenever they attempt to monitor employees as they engage in their protected concerted activities. This is known as *unlawful surveillance*.

As employees increasingly use various forms of social media to communicate and express thoughts about their jobs and their workplaces, employers have stepped up their monitoring of such activities. When employers see what they perceive to be disloyal or disparaging comments by their employees as expressed in social media, they sometimes impose job discipline measures up to and including termination.

In recent years, the National Labor Relations Board (NLRB) has aggressively expanded its enforcement activities against employers who have sought to engage in surveillance of employees' use of social media and to otherwise quash protected concerted activity. Thus, employers who use Big Data analytics aimed at identifying employees' thoughts and perceptions about themselves, their jobs, and their workplaces may run afoul of the NLRA.

The NLRB has gone after employers who have taken disciplinary action against an employee based on that employee's Facebook postings critical of the employer. In a case involving a BMW auto dealer in suburban Chicago, the employer terminated one of its auto sales reps because his Facebook posting implied the employer was cheap, presumably because it served only hot dogs and chips during a new model event held at the dealership, whereas a competitor Mercedes dealer provided hors d'oeuvres served by waiters. Although ultimately the discharge of the sales rep was upheld, the NLRB found in that case, as it has in a number of others, employers who have broad policies against negative social media postings will run afoul of the act's guarantee of all employees to engage in protected concerted activity, even where no union exists.[18] Thus, any Big Data analytic that monitors employees' use of social media, like Facebook or Twitter, should avoid analyzing comments about the workplace or terms and conditions (wages and benefits) of their employment. Because the law under the NLRA tends to be very fact specific, employers who in any way seek to survey or monitor the use of social media as part of gathering Big Data analytics about their employees or organization will be well advised to consult both the current case law under the NLRA and various case law compendiums issued by the general counsel of the NLRB.

In implementing social media policies for its employees, all employers must carefully consider the laws on employee privacy as well as the latest pronouncements from the NLRB. Nonunion employers who previously never considered NLRB ramifications need to fully understand and consider the latest pronouncements from the NLRB before disciplining or discharging any employee for alleged improper use of social media. Given the NLRB's increased enforcement of employees' right to engage in protected concerted activity, even nonunion employers must be prepared to defend against potential charges filed with the NLRB by aggrieved employees.

10.7 FAIR CREDIT REPORTING ACT

Increasingly, employers are using background checks of candidates' criminal records and credit histories as part of the interview and hiring process.

The use of such checks is regulated by the federal Fair Credit Reporting Act and is discussed in detail in Chapter 4, "Privacy and Big Data."

10.8 STATE AND LOCAL LAWS

There are a multitude of state and local laws, too numerous to discuss in this chapter, that replicate those discussed previously; often, these go further than the federal standards. Managers must consider these when using Big Data analytics to manage their human resources.

10.9 CONCLUSION

The human resource function is one area that stands to greatly enhance the quality of business decisions through the use of Big Data. The legal framework that regulates the employment process must be considered but should not be seen as a barrier to the use of Big Data. Like many other areas of data management, the law lags the technology, which makes compliance more difficult, but not impossible. Through careful planning, Big Data analytics can take human resource management to a new capability level.

NOTES

1. Sharlyn Lauby. Human Resources Adding Value to the Company. December 16, 2012. Available at http://www.HRBartender.com.
2. Edward E. Lawler III. *Pay and Organizational Effectiveness: A Psychological View.* McGraw-Hill, New York, 1971.
3. Daniel R. Pink. *Drive.* Riverhead, New York, 2009.
4. Flu Trends: How Does It Work? 2011. Available at http://www.google.org/flutrends/about/how.html.
5. Declan Butler. When Google Got Flu Wrong. *Nature,* February 13, 2013. Available at http://www.nature.com/news/when-google-got-flu-wrong-1.12413.
6. New Methods for Real-Time Influenza Forecasting Appeared Effective. *Infectious Disease News,* December 20, 2013. Available at http://www.healio.com/infectious-disease/influenza/news/online/%7B9183c557-f289-496c-8a5e-f19d2314b77a%7D/new-methods-for-real-time-influenza-forecasting-appeared-effective.
7. Joseph Walker. Meet the New Boss Big Data. *Wall Street Journal,* September 20, 2012. Available at http://online.wsj.com/news/articles/SB10000872396390443890304578006252019616768 (subscription required).

8. Don Peck. They're Watching You at Work. *The Atlantic*, December 2013.

9. Rachel King. Data Helps Firms Find the Right Workers for the Right Jobs. *Wall Street Journal*, September 15, 2013. Available at http://online.wsj.com/news/articles/SB100 01424127887323906804579036573250528100 (subscription required).

10. Lamar Pierce, Daniel C. Snow, and Andrew McAfee. Cleaning House; The Impact of Information Technology Monitoring on Employee Theft and Productivity. MIT Sloan Research Paper No. 5029-13. November 12, 2013. Available at http://papers.ssrn.com/sol3/papers.cfm?abstract_id=2318592.

11. 42 U.S.C. 2000(e) et seq.

12. *Griggs v. Duke Power Company*, 401 U.S. 424 (1971).

13. 29 C.F.R. Part 1607.

14. 29 U.S.C. § 2000ff et seq.

15. 42 U.S.C. 2705(j)(1)(A).

16. 42 U.S.C. 300gg-4(a), (j), and (m).

17. 42 U.S.C. 2000ff–1(b)(2).

18. Karl Knauz Motors, Inc., 358 NLRB No. 164 (Sept. 28, 2012).

11

Big Data Discovery

Adam C. Losey

11.1 INTRODUCTION

In this chapter, you will learn

- About the duty to preserve electronic evidence and how it has an impact on Big Data;
- How to prevent common mistakes in preserving electronic evidence;
- Common litigation hold triggers and how to spot and address Big Data preservation triggers that you might otherwise overlook;
- The value of weaving automated preservation processes into Big Data analytics to ensure legal compliance, to protect corporate information, and to reduce risk;
- How to effectively address, seek, and combat database discovery;
- About clawback orders and how to use them to protect privilege; and
- How to cost-effectively and efficiently review Big Data in the context of discovery requests by using computer-assisted review (CAR).

11.2 BIG DATA, BIG PRESERVATION PROBLEMS

The large data collections inherent in Big Data analysis have operational and strategic value. But, the preservation, collection, search, and review of Big Data can create big problems in the discovery process in litigation, starting before a lawsuit is even filed.

As of 2014, of all data in the world, 90% was created in the past two years, per IBM Analytics.[1] Amounts of information previously unimaginable in size can now be stored for a relatively low cost. As an example, for less than $100, you can purchase a 2-terabyte hard drive, which holds 2,048 gigabytes. Assuming that 1 gigabyte holds about 100,000 printed pages of text (a conservative estimate), this $90 hard drive can easily hold 204,800,000 pages of text—about a 1.3-mile tall stack of paper if printed and plopped into a pen-and-ink inbox (see Figure 1.1, "Visualizing Big Data").

Assume a lawyer can review one digital page of text a minute—a brisk pace. It will take the lawyer 20 years of daily 8-hour days (including weekends) to review the data that can be stored on this 2-terabyte hard drive. Even at extremely low hourly rates, using fixed fees or an offshore service, the review cost would be staggering. To put it in perspective, the amount of data that can be stored on a hard drive for about a nickel could cost hundreds of thousands of dollars for human eyes-on review.

This ratio of storage cost to review cost is the core of the electronic discovery problem facing modern litigants. The volume problem is made worse when coupled with the fact that most modern businesses have all sorts of different types of electronically stored information (from texts, to voice mails, to Internet Protocol logs) residing in hundreds or thousands of separate locations. Frequently, no one person at a company will truly know where all the relevant data resides. An attorney cannot simply ask a client to search for all files on a matter and meet applicable legal requirements for discovery due diligence. From preservation, to collection, search, and review, twentieth-century discovery methodologies must be adapted to handle twenty-first-century discovery in this era of Big Data.

11.3 BIG DATA PRESERVATION

11.3.1 The Duty to Preserve: A Time-Tested Legal Doctrine Meets Big Data

In our legal system, once a person or business reasonably anticipates litigation, they generally have a duty to preserve information relevant to the reasonably anticipated litigation. This includes incriminating (and privileged) evidence that is harmful to the preserving party, as well as information that might be helpful. The preservation duty, to some extent, runs contrary to human nature and puts the litigant in the awkward position of being charged to take care to maintain information and data both harmful and helpful to the litigant's cause. This has been the common law for hundreds of years, and spoliation (the destruction of evidence that a party had a duty to preserve) has been an issue all the way back to Dickensian England (see *Armory v. Delamirie*, 93 Eng. Rep. 664 (K.B. 1722)).[2]

Requiring a person to keep something harmful to their own cause runs contrary to a human tendency to want to prevent incriminating evidence, whether electronic or otherwise, from seeing the light of day. As a result, unfortunately, spoliation has been and remains a common issue in litigation. Because of the ability to conduct forensic analysis on hard drives and other sources of electronically stored information (as well as the proliferation of electronically stored information), it is now easier to detect and prove spoliation.

The duty to preserve requires corporate and outside counsel to educate clients on the duty to preserve and to shepherd clients through the preservation process. This process runs the gamut from deciding when the duty to preserve is triggered to ensuring that data is actually preserved. Given the exponential increase in amount of data and the diffuse and distributed nature of most network infrastructures, this is no easy feat. The stakes are high. The failure to preserve data once the duty to preserve is triggered has serious consequences. Spoliation sanctions, those levied based on the destruction of evidence, range widely and can result in a party losing litigation by default. Spoliation sanctions can come about simply by allowing critical data to be lost by operation of automated processes after the preservation duty has triggered.

A recent example involving automatic deletion of data leading to sanctions involved an employment claim.[3] The plaintiff, Pillay, alleged that Millard, the refrigeration company he worked for, fired an employee named Ramirez because Millard believed Ramirez to be disabled, and then that Pillay was fired for complaining to Millard about Ramirez's alleged wrongful termination.

Millard used a labor management system called "LMS[,]" to track its employees' productivity and performance using performance analytics. In this case, Millard relied on LMS data to justify the termination of Ramirez and Pillay. Pillay argued that Millard regularly manipulated the LMS data and propounded discovery for the underlying LMS data to attempt to prove discrimination and manipulation of the LMS data. Pillay then learned that the LMS data was gone. How did this happen?

Pillay was fired in August 2008. In December 2008, Pillay's attorney advised Millard "to preserve evidence and documents," including electronic communications or data related to his client's employment, specifically citing "[a]ll communications, documents, emails, or anything relating to Mr. Ramirez's productivity and work evaluations." In July 2010, Millard notified Pillay that the data used to calculate Ramirez's LMS numbers had been deleted. Millard explained that "the discrete data [that formulates LMS numbers] is automatically deleted after one year" to keep its system operating at an optimal level. Apparently, no one at Millard flipped the "off" switch for the automated purge process, and no one bothered to archive the salient data for Ramirez and Pillay.

11.3.2 Avoiding Preservation Pitfalls

Pillay successfully moved for a spoliation inference based on the charge that Millard had destroyed critical evidence—a classic case of a company facing consequences from failing to take steps to avoid automated system purge processes. This is but one of many oft-seen preservation blunders. The following is a list of the top five common preservation pitfalls and how you can avoid them.

11.3.2.1 Failure to Flip the Off Switch

Most companies use some automatic deletion or overwrite policies or protocols to manage various types of data. Things like Internet Protocol (IP) logs, which detail access to computer systems, and Big Data troves (such as the LMS system in *Pillay*) are routinely overwritten after set retention periods as a matter of course. The same is true with emails and electronic files that have no business or regulatory compliance value. This automated deletion as part of a document retention and system optimization policy is generally fine and even protected under certain federal and state laws. For example, Federal Rule of Civil Procedure 37(e) provides that "[a]bsent exceptional circumstances, a court may not impose sanctions under these rules on a party for failing to provide electronically stored information lost as a result of the routine, good-faith operation of an electronic information system." But, these protections do not allow deletion of data once the preservation duty triggers. How do you prevent automatic deletion blunders? Loop information technology personnel into the electronic evidence preservation process and take the time to educate them about the legal requirements. Ensure your counsel understands the nature of various sources of electronically stored information and where and how data is stored. Know what needs to be done to flip the off switch on any automatic deletion protocols for relevant information. Document that preservation steps have been taken regarding any evidence in question. If you choose not to stop the automated processes, alternate means to effectively preserve the evidence should be used; for example, you can typically export and archive the salient data. In the *Pillay* case, Millard could have at least archived Ramirez's LMS data and kept the automatic deletion policy in place. This holds true even beyond the automated deletion example. For example, reissuing laptops from former employees to new employees and wiping the old information (which is the norm in many companies) can also lead to sanctions. "Once a 'litigation hold' has been established, a party cannot continue a routine procedure that effectively ensures that potentially relevant and readily available information is no longer 'reasonably accessible.'" [4] Do not rely on information technology staff to understand what is or is not relevant to a claim; that is a legal judgment that should be left to lawyers. Conversely, corporate or outside counsel may not have the experience to know how corporate information systems function. Consequently, effective preservation requires open and frequent communication between information technology personnel, the business personnel, and counsel.

11.3.2.2 The Spreadsheet Error

Typically, companies send out litigation hold notices to individual custodians and information technology personnel letting them know to preserve information relevant to a claim and containing specific instructions particular to a claim. Tracking these litigation holds can be a challenge for large companies and in large litigations. When a company has a dozen or more litigations, each with potentially dozens of custodians and sources of information, keeping track of whose information was preserved, who received a hold, and where preserved information resides presents opportunities for error. The same can be true with a single large litigation; for example, it is not uncommon to have tens of thousands of custodians in a Fair Labor Standards Act class action and to have dozens of nonparties in control of data relevant to claims (e.g., payroll companies, cloud computing services, reimbursement vendors). In particular, when Excel spreadsheets are used to track litigation holds by manual data input, mistakes frequently happen. Through human error, spoliation can occur because the wrong data is entered into the wrong column or row (i.e., "yes" is entered on the wrong custodian for a field "sent litigation hold[,]" and as a result the custodian is never sent a hold and the data is lost). The solution? Buy or build a scalable litigation hold tracking solution that automates as much of the process as possible; including

- Who received hold notices, what they contained, and when they were issued;
- Calendaring follow-ups to custodians who do not respond to holds;
- Monitoring and documenting preservation efforts, including what was preserved, who preserved it, where the data resides, and when it was preserved;
- Other steps taken to alert individuals to their preservation responsibilities, including automated system modifications; and
- Use of multiple providers that offer low-cost off-the-shelf litigation hold tracking solutions. Custom solutions are also an option, but these are typically more expensive. These systems should ideally be put in place before litigation occurs, as addressing the new system while a preservation obligation is in place is typically not an optimal environment to vet various products and options for use on a company-wide basis.

11.3.2.3 The Never-Ending Hold

The duty to preserve does not extend in perpetuity. It ends once the reasonable anticipation of litigation ends, which can occur after settlement, at the conclusion of the litigation and after the time period to file a notice of appeal has passed, or at the end of a statute of limitations for a claim. Yet, more often than not, litigation hold notices are forgotten about and never lifted even after the duty to preserve has ended. This is wasteful as often this litigation data has no business or compliance value. Waste aside, litigation holds can be headaches for individual employees—keeping everything related to a topic requires time and attention and can drain productivity that can otherwise be spent fulfilling business functions. Thus, you do not want to have a hold in place any longer than necessary. The solution is to make sure your litigation hold process includes a mechanism to lift holds when appropriate. This process should not be reliant on an individual, if possible, as individuals tend to come and go from employment because of typical attrition or the engagement of different counsel; typically, litigation hold tracking solutions include features to help ensure holds are eventually lifted.

11.3.2.4 The Fire and Forget

Many litigation holds are completely ignored by the recipients. Too often, companies and counsel see sending the litigation hold as a "fire-and-forget" task that is necessary to eliminate from a checklist, forgetting the ultimate point of a litigation hold: to ensure the recipients actually preserve the information in a timely manner. Simply sending the letter often does not accomplish this task: "[i]t is not sufficient . . . for a company merely to tell employees to 'save relevant documents.' . . . This sort of token effort will hardly ever suffice."[5] To ensure that holds are followed, make sure to

- Send timely, routine follow-ups and contact key personnel to ensure that they have read and will comply with the hold;
- Engage directly with information technology personnel to ensure that necessary information is actually collected;
- Set deadlines for preservation and collection tasks for information technology personnel and ensure those deadlines are met;
- Ask information technology personnel to send or preserve data to a specific location—and then verify the data is accessible and readable from that location;
- Engage supervisory personnel or management in the litigation hold process; typically, employees pay close attention to correspondence when it comes from someone higher up in the organization, and having holds come from key personnel (or even cc'ing key personnel) can be helpful in encouraging compliance; and
- Use telephone and in-person follow-ups with recipients, where feasible, which go a long way to encouraging compliance. Where feasible, picking up the phone at the outset to explain the process and the urgency of compliance is one of the best methods of encouraging employees to take the required steps.

11.3.2.5 Deputizing Custodians as Information Technology Personnel

Frequently, individual custodians are relied on to collect and preserve their own electronically stored information. Employees are thus deputized as information technology personnel and lawyers and charged with manually selecting and harvesting data relevant to a claim. This practice has been criticized both as a "fox guarding the henhouse," whereby custodial self-bias would lead to withholding of incriminating information, and as requiring rank-and-file employees to jump in over their heads concerning the technical requirements of collection. In many cases, employees would not even have access to the tools that system administrators would have for preservation. For example, on a Microsoft Exchange Server, typically only an administrator can flag an account on "litigation hold" and prevent the deletion of email, which could also preserve emails that were deleted previously by the custodian. Finally, custodial self-collection can be distracting and detrimental to a business; if you do not know what you are doing, it can be time consuming and frustrating to try to collect and preserve electronically stored information. Although custodial self-collection is not prohibited by law in most circumstances, it is typically not the best practice for these reasons. The solution is simply to loop in information technology personnel to accomplish collection and to use information technology employees or experienced vendors to collect data. For small companies, many forensic companies offer relatively low-cost "plug-and-collect" devices so even technologically unsophisticated employees or managers can simply plug in a device and allow the device to automatically conduct forensically sound data collection.

11.3.3 Pulling the Litigation Hold Trigger

Although the *Pillay* case involved a clear trigger date of duty to preserve (i.e., Millard was on notice that the LMS data was relevant when it deleted the data), the reasonable anticipation of litigation standard is inherently ambiguous. The judicial determination of when a company reasonably anticipates litigation necessarily involves a subjective after-the-fact analysis by a judge or jury.

In the absence of an obvious bright-line litigation hold triggering event, such as the filing or service of a complaint, a court will consider a variety of variables to determine when this preservation duty arises. From a judicial standpoint, this variability is desirable, despite the potential for inconsistency. Attempts to produce clarity and uniformity through the imposition of a forced bright-line test could cause unnecessary rigidity in the preservation standard.

For example, a uniform rule that a party need only preserve data after it was sued or filed suit would create an opportunity for mischief (i.e., pre-suit "housecleaning" of incriminating data).[6] However, for organizations, individuals, and their lawyers, this malleability makes it difficult to determine whether a litigation threat or an event is serious enough to trigger information preservation obligations.

The preservation duty is certainly triggered by the service of a lawsuit on a party; if you are sued and served, you obviously know litigation is happening. The old paradigm typically involves an event-specific analysis of the duty to preserve that most lawyers would recognize as potential litigation triggers. For example, an employee allegedly physically confronting a supervisor,[7] a fatal accident,[8] a notice that food products were contaminated,[9] the service or filing of a complaint, or a plaintiff's retention of counsel to sue are all recognizable and chronologically specific events that have triggered the duty to preserve.

Big Data brings the potential for a less-obvious and new paradigm on the reasonable anticipation of litigation standard. If a company has the resources and can use people and technology to quickly analyze large amounts of data of different types from a variety of sources to produce a stream of actionable knowledge, there is a question of how this heightened insight affects the preservation duty.

11.3.4 Big Data Preservation Triggers

The LMS system in the *Pillay* case provides an excellent example of the potential for a new Big Data preservation paradigm. The system measured productivity of employees, and this type of analytic tool can have an impact on the determination of when litigation is anticipated and a data hold is required. Predictive analytics of employee timekeeping records, productivity records, email accounts, and even Internet search history can also show when employees spend a large percentage of their time on personal or nonwork matters (e.g., sending a high volume of personal emails on the clock, shopping online, bantering about fantasy football).

Companies pay employees to work, not to dither online. Analytics that detect personal activity on company time to measure productivity are simultaneously identifying grounds for employee discipline or termination. Spending frequent time on the clock while browsing personal websites or shopping for personal items online can be a ground for termination. Employee productivity data analytics can then give rise to preservation obligations, and preservation of data that provides grounds for termination in an employment context is doubly important, as *Pillay* illustrates. The records showing an employee's on-the-clock activity need to be kept in a manner that they can be used as evidence later and, where appropriate, need to be routed to counsel so they can make the legal determination of whether the analytic data triggers the legal duty to preserve.

Employee behavior analytics can also detect when employees are likely sending trade secret or confidential information outside the company. Large amounts of emails with multiple attachments sent in rapid succession, frequently without any information in the subject line or the text, are often a sign of a document grab for personal or competitive use. The behavior is typical, as most employees keep documents on a company system, computer, or hard drive, and many times employees attempt to download or transmit this information en masse is prior to leaving employment or seeking to sell the information to a competitor. More technologically sophisticated employees typically attempt to cover their tracks by using flash drives or attempting to delete sent items to avoid leaving easily trackable electronic trails, but even sophisticated employees who try to cover their tracks typically leave a followable trail of electronic evidence. In an exemplar case involving data theft, the day before an employee's employment with the company was terminated, he "forwarded [confidential and trade secret information from his workplace] email to his personal email account, and that he used the information to recruit additional employees and agents on behalf of [a competitor]."[10] This is, unfortunately, typical employee behavior.

Certainly large-scale document grabs for personal or competitive use not only are a ground for termination but also may require immediate attention by counsel to preserve and retrieve the confidential information. Once trade secret or confidential information escapes, it is difficult to mitigate the harm and to prevent the data from being used. Preventing the use or sale of proprietary and valuable information such as customer lists or trade secret data requires fast action. A preliminary injunction or other quick provisional remedy may be needed to prevent the use of the information and contain the damage.

As another example, the casualty insurance industry often provides insurance for individual or organizational negligent acts or omissions. As you may imagine, litigation costs and the potential for litigation are major factors in handling casualty claims. Because of this, some casualty insurers use Big Data techniques in applying litigation prediction applications to their claims system. This predictive know-how can help control claim costs, but it can also trigger the duty to preserve at a much earlier date.

For example, say an insurer received a claim request. This in itself would not necessarily trigger the duty to preserve because the receipt of an insurance claim without more may not mean that litigation is on the horizon. Many insurance claims resolve short of litigation. However, assume this same insurer received a claim request and using predictive analytics determined that there is a 20% chance that the claim will result in litigation. This data-driven knowledge could trigger the duty to preserve.

A litigation threat rising to the level of "reasonable anticipation" requires more than the mere possibility that litigation might occur.[11] Litigation must actually be, to some extent, likely. The reasonable anticipation standard is also applied by lawyers, and lawyers are typically quicker than nonlawyers to see litigation lurking around every corner. A lawyer or judge may see an empty playground with no fencing around the playground, think "attractive nuisance[,]" and reason that the owner of the playground should reasonably anticipate litigation. A layman would more likely just see a swing set and would not equate an unfenced playground to a likely litigation risk.

At the 20% probability level, it is entirely possible that a court would hold that this percentage chance rose to the level of reasonable anticipation of litigation. At a 50% or greater level, it is likely that a court would find that the knowledge gleaned from the Big Data analytics created a reasonable anticipation of litigation on behalf of the casualty insurer. Although there is no set percentage threshold uniformly applied across the country as the minimum threshold for reasonable anticipation of litigation, whenever Big Data analytics are used, you should do the following:

- **Loop in the Lawyers.** If your Big Data analysis involves employee performance, loop in a labor and employment lawyer to discuss what obligations you may have in conjunction with preservation. For insurance analytics, loop in an insurance lawyer for the same reason. Consult a legal subject matter expert in the early phases regarding whatever it is your analytic tool measures to determine what the potential compliance and legal obligations surrounding the analytic tool may be and implement measures to preserve data or offer input on the analytic process that are recommended by counsel.
- **Be Sure You Want and Need to Know.** As far back as 2009, two seniors at the Massachusetts Institute of Technology (MIT) conducted a study whereby they were able to create an effective "method

of classifying sexual orientation of individuals on Facebook, regardless of whether they chose to disclose that information. Facebook users who did not disclose their sexual orientation in their profiles would presumably consider the present research an invasion of privacy. Yet this research uses nothing more than information already publicly provided on Facebook; no interaction with subjects was required."[12] While an interesting study in data analytics, no corporate human resources department would condone this type of tool being used in the hiring process. Certainly, a plaintiff would argue that there would be no possible legitimate use of this tool in the workplace, and that any rationale given would be a pretext for discrimination. Thus, make sure you want to know—and have a need to know—whatever it is you are seeking to extract from Big Data.

- **Automate Preservation.** Assuming you consult with counsel and determine your Big Data analytics could trigger preservation obligations, automate preservation to the extent possible. For example, if an employee's productivity level were to drop below whatever a company deemed the lowest threshold, that employee's email account could be automatically flagged on litigation hold, the employee's Internet history saved permanently (to check to see if he or she was browsing the web on company time), and phone records and other documentation saved. Automating these functions takes out the lag time associated with human beings, as well as eliminates the room for error associated with human involvement in manual input tasks.

- **Be Quick.** Particularly with data protection analytics targeted to employees, counsel needs to be alerted quickly to take the necessary triage actions, as well as preserve data relevant to the employee's actions. Access logs and other data showing access to systems typically are overwritten on a regular basis, and preserving this information that has a short shelf life can be crucial in claims involving theft of confidential or trade secret information. Assuming automated processes are used that preserve information immediately on analytics hitting on a risk, immediate response time is readily achievable. Assuming human beings are used, steps need to be taken to ensure extremely fast response time to triage situations that ensure that you have appropriate time to act to stop the release or mitigate its impacts. If predictive analytics key on an employee theft of trade secret information or a data breach but aggressive steps, including seeking an injunction, are not taken immediately, that delay can be the difference between obtaining a court order to seize the data from the employee, notifying a bank of stolen credit card numbers quickly, or being faced with a Snowden-like situation in which the company information has been made public and the harm from disclosure is exponentially increased.

11.4 BIG DATABASE DISCOVERY

Big database discovery can also present problems. Big Data analytics can be based on structured data, frequently contained in databases. Large structured databases present a number of challenges in discovery. Working with structured data (such as that contained in a traditional database) is different from working with unstructured data (such as a series of Word documents in a folder).

11.4.1 The Database Difference

Databases contain discrete categories of information, divided into individual fields. These structured categories of information are kept together collectively. The individual database fields in structured databases differ from typical unstructured data because, unlike unstructured data, structured data is typically not presented in the exact form that it was created. Rather, structured databases are composites of fields that only make sense through their interrelationship. Structured databases also typically have tightly defined parameters regarding how data is input, kept, and retrieved. As an example, a structured database may break a location into multiple elements that do not make sense when broken apart. The coordinates 34°59′20 N, 106°36′52 W refer to a specific location, but a structured database would store each numeral as a discrete element (34, 59, 20, 106, 36, and 52), with each element stored in a separate data field. Unlike a Word document or an Excel spreadsheet, each of these separate elements must refer to the others to make sense; only collectively are they coordinates as opposed to a numerical jumble.

The preservation of structured databases is challenging because most databases are active composites of various information. To put a "hold" on the use or modification of the database itself could be crippling to a business in which the database is used constantly to fulfill critical business functions. The structure of the database and its contents typically guide the methods used to ensure that relevant data is preserved. But, in the context of Big Data, limitation on the scope of preservation is particularly important. Simply because certain fields in a structured database are relevant does not mean the entire database is within the scope of the duty to preserve.

11.4.2 Databases in Litigation

Case law generally supports that a litigant will not gain access to another's database simply because some of the data within a database is relevant to litigation, and typically parties will confer regarding targeted queries as opposed to wholesale production. Many databases contain personally identifiable information subject to data protection laws, as well as confidential or trade secret information.

Under the applicable Federal Rules of Civil Procedure, a litigant does not automatically receive unrestricted, direct access to a party's database compilations. Instead, a requesting party can inspect and copy data relevant to the lawsuit.[13]

It is, however, possible to gain access to a database directly in the correct circumstances. A recent example of database litigation in a trademark infringement and fraud case resulted in just this type of access.[14] The plaintiff in this case obtained a temporary restraining order against the defendants and sought expedited discovery in the form of a copy of defendants' OS Commerce database. The defendants alleged this database contained individual fields congruent to sales information about products ordered and sold and contained allegedly sensitive information (such as listings of the defendants' customers).

The defendants objected to allowing access to the database, claiming that the request asked for confidential and sensitive information from its "most important asset" that would give the plaintiff a competitive advantage and that the request amounted to "an obvious fishing expedition." Reasoning that the information on the database was highly relevant, the court held that "although [the plaintiff's] request for [the defendant's] entire OS Commerce database appears facially intrusive, the benefits of allowing [plaintiff] such direct access, under the circumstances of this case, outweigh the burden of producing it, particularly since a protective order is in place. . . . [Access to the database] is more than a mere fishing expedition." As the *Advanced Tactical* case showed, database discovery parameters are determined by the facts of the individual case—what is impermissible in one case may be perfectly permissible in the next. So, how do you handle database preservation, collection, and search?

11.4.3 Cooperate Where You Can

Many database discovery disputes escalate unnecessarily because of a lack of technological understanding by counsel on both sides of the aisle.[15] Frequently, expensive discovery disputes can be resolved when counsel consult with individuals in information technology about the capabilities for database exports and understand the unique issues associated with database production. When responding to discovery, rather than fight over wholesale database production, explain why wholesale production does not make sense and talk about the various database fields from which you can export to come to a reasonable solution for an export and production. When seeking discovery, ask about the fields in the database and determine what you need. Do not ask for more than you need, and if you want direct access to the database, agree to confidentiality safeguards and reasonable measures in exchange for supervised direct access.

11.4.4 Object to Unreasonable Demands

State and federal courts across the country are attuned to the idea of proportionality in eDiscovery: A $100,000 claim does not typically justify $100,000 in eDiscovery expense. The Federal Rules of Civil Procedure provide for proportionality, and although there is no magic percentage number universally blessed by the courts (i.e., 1% of the claim amount is reasonable for discovery), high-dollar database preservation or production requests that impose an undue burden should be resisted. Try to cooperate and reach a reasonable middle ground, but refuse to comply and lodge the appropriate objections to unreasonable and unduly expensive preservation or production demands. Get before a judge if possible. Failure to object can have disastrous consequences, such as being forced to pay approximately $6 million to comply with a nonparty subpoena.[16]

11.4.5 Be Specific

The *Advanced Tactical* defendants were criticized for submitting information to the court about their database in "rather general terms[,]" as it was difficult for the court to make a reasoned decision in a fact-specific analysis with only general information about the information systems involved. This is an extremely common failing in eDiscovery litigation, in that counsel will typically speak in generalities—that is, "the request is too burdensome" as opposed to "the request requires the review of 1,234,522 email documents, 1,234 Word documents, and 2,234 voice mail messages, which would cost approximately X dollars and Y work hours, which is overly burdensome." Specific information justifying why data should or should not be produced needs to be presented to the court to win eDiscovery disputes. The *Advanced Tactical* plaintiff, for example, provided a specific reason why they alleged they needed direct database access, arguing that "once it has the database, it can determine whether, as it has reason to suspect, [defendant] is using hidden 'metatags' referencing [the plaintiff's] trademark 'pepperball' to drive higher search engine results for that term." In *Advanced Tactical*, the plaintiff prevailed, and specific and salient facts must be presented to the Court to enable the court to reach a reasoned decision.

11.4.6 Talk about Database Discovery Early in the Process

In the federal system, parties are required to meet and confer on eDiscovery in their Rule 26(f) conference, and many states have equivalent mandatory meet and confer requirements. Talking about database discovery early on is the best way to address and resolve all the various issues, as frequently counsel shy away from even admitting to having databases that could be subject to search. Hiding from issues or attempting to hide the ball on sources of information is a bad solution that typically ends in increased litigation expense for all parties; do not be afraid to bring up the issue at the outset of discovery. If there is a good-faith disagreement on scope of preservation or production, the court can become involved and resolve the dispute early in the process, before discovery is conducted, to prevent discovery redos or slipups.

11.5 BIG DATA DIGGING

Much as Big Data involves the use of predictive analytics to derive insights from large datasets, CAR enables lawyers to use active machine learning algorithms to review large document sets in litigation. Active machine learning is a type of artificial intelligence. When used in legal search, these artificial intelligence algorithms can significantly improve the efficiency and accuracy in the search, review, and classification of electronically stored information.

11.5.1 Driving the CAR Process

Using CAR, an attorney or group of attorneys trains a computer to find documents identified by the attorney or group as a target. The target is typically relevant to a particular lawsuit or legal issue, or some other legal classification, such as privilege. The CAR system acts as a force multiplier for senior attorney judgment, allowing (in the correct case) better recall and precision in the search while reducing overall costs. CAR works well on text-searchable datasets of discrete information, particularly so on email. The classic example of a CAR-amenable dataset is a large number of emails, accompanied by various loose unstructured data collections, such as Word documents, Adobe portable document format (PDF) files, and the like.

First, a subject matter expert (or experts) on the case performs manual reviews of search samples from the dataset. The samples are selected by the attorney's judgment, and are not random samples. The selections are made with the help of various software search features, including keyword searches and concept searches. Then, statistically random sampling is used to establish a baseline for quality control purposes.

Next, the CAR software's calculations begin. This is also known as seed set training. Here, the predictive coding software analyzes all of the categorizations made by subject matter experts in the prior steps as long as the documents were designated by them as training documents. Based on this input, coding runs begin by which the software scans all of the data uploaded onto a review platform (the corpus) and assigns a probable value from 0 to 100 to each document in the corpus. A value of 100 represents the highest probability (100%) that the document matches the category trained, such as relevant, or highly relevant; a value of 0 means no likelihood of matching, whereas 50 represents equal likelihood. The software predictions about a document's categorization are often wrong, sometimes wildly so, depending on the kind of search and data involved. This is why spot-checking and further training are needed for CAR to work properly: It is an iterative process, not a one-step automated review.

After the initial categorization is completed, prediction error corrections are made. Lawyers and paralegals find and correct the computer errors by a variety of methods. The CAR software learns from the corrections. This iterative process is repeated in a virtuous feedback loop that continues until the computer predictions are accurate enough to satisfy discovery standards.

Next, the reasonability of the decision to stop the training is evaluated by an objective quality control test. The test is based on a random sample of all documents to be excluded from the final review for possible production. The exclusion can be based on both category prediction (i.e., probable irrelevant) and probable ranking of document with proportionate cutoffs. The focus is on a search for any false negatives (i.e., relevant documents incorrectly predicted to be irrelevant) that are relevant or otherwise of significance.

The decision is then made on the number of documents to be reviewed by humans for possible production. Typically, a litigant will use CAR processes to winnow out irrelevant documents and will then have humans review the documents identified by the CAR process as relevant. But, this is not always the case, as sometimes a litigant will produce the documents using keyword searches or other methods to spot-check samples of the produced documents.

Finally, after all the documents are reviewed, they are typically spot-checked and produced. The final work includes preparation of a privilege log, which is typically delayed until after production. Also, large-scale productions are frequently done in rolling stages as review is completed.

11.5.2 The Clawback

When using CAR methods, because of the volume of data involved, litigants should use clawback orders as a matter of course to help protect from privilege waiver in large-scale productions. According to District Court Judge Browning, "[t]he train on th[e] concept [of clawback orders] has already left the station, and clawback orders are staples of modern complex commercial litigation."[17]

What is a clawback order, you might ask, and why did Judge Browning drop this locomotive metaphor? In the *S2 Automation* opinion, Judge Browning quoted Professor James Moore's concise rundown of a clawback order:

Federal courts may enter confidentiality orders providing that disclosure of privileged or protected material in a litigation pending before the court does not constitute waiver in other state or federal proceedings. In suggesting this provision, the Advisory Committee acknowledged that the utility of a confidentiality order in reducing discovery costs is substantially diminished if it provides no protection outside the particular litigation in which the order is entered. Entry of a confidentiality order will prevent nonparties to the litigation from obtaining privileged material produced pursuant to such a confidentiality order. The rule also encompasses situations in which the parties are ordered to provide documents under a "claw-back" or "quick peek" arrangement. These types of arrangements allow the parties to produce documents for review and return without engaging in a privilege review, but without waiver of privilege or work product protection, as a way to avoid the excessive costs of full privilege review and disclosure when large numbers of documents are involved. The rule provides the parties with predicable protection from waiver when responding to a court order for production of documents pursuant to such an arrangement.

A clawback order is essentially a privilege waiver prophylactic. Federal Rule of Evidence 502(d) gives a federal court the power to enter this kind of clawback order, and as the advisory committee notes to 502(d) indicate, the parties do not even have to agree on the clawback order for the court to enter it. The advisory committee also correctly pointed out that such orders "are becoming increasingly important in limiting the costs of privilege review and retention, especially in cases involving electronic discovery[.]" Judge Browning's case involved a situation where the plaintiff just "[did] not like the overall concept" (for whatever reason), and the court held that "[t]he train on that concept has already left the station, and clawback orders are staples of modern complex commercial litigation." The lesson? Do not try to stop the clawback train. Instead, get on board, and sleep a little easier about privilege waiver. These types of clawback arrangements can also allow the parties to produce documents for review and return without engaging in a full-scale privilege review, but without waiver of privilege or work product protection, as a way to avoid the excessive costs of full privilege review and disclosure when large numbers of documents are involved.

Although typically lawyers rightly cringe at the thought of cursory privilege review, bottom-line considerations can trump the legal best practice; disclosing privileged documents (without waiving privilege) can be a more attractive situation than spending additional sums on privilege review to ensure withholding of privileged documentation. Even with full-scale privilege review, when millions of emails are in play, accidental production of privileged material is statistically likely, and the clawback rule provides the parties with predicable protection from waiver when responding to a court order for production of documents pursuant to such an arrangement.

11.6 JUDICIAL ACCEPTANCE OF CAR METHODS

When CAR began to see more widespread use a few years ago, litigants occasionally sparred over the use of the technology in lieu of straight eyes-on-every-document review. Then, the first judicial opinion endorsing the use of CAR came in *Da Silva Moore v. Publicis Groupe*, 287 F.R.D. 102 (S.D.N.Y. 2012). *Da Silva* was a lengthy and hotly contested case for which the court dug deeply into the inner working of the CAR process.

Since *Da Silva*, there have been a number of concise opinions or excerpts of state court judges accepting the concept of CAR as the norm. A Virginia state court endorsed the use of CAR, over strenuous objection, in a partially handwritten order in *Global Aero. Inc. v. Landow Aviation, L.P.*, 2012 Va. Cir. LEXIS 50 (Va. Cir. Ct., Apr. 23, 2012).

In the Southern District of New York, Judges Kaplan and Treece have both cited the availability of CAR as part of their analysis in rejecting undue burden objections to discovery requests. As another recent example of CAR acceptance from a December 2012 hearing at which the use of CAR was challenged, Judge Andrews in Delaware stated:

> Why isn't that something—you know, you answered their discovery however you answered it—why isn't it something where they answer your discovery however they choose to answer it, complying with their professional obligations? How do you get to be involved in the seed batch?[18]

Thus, the evolving attitude seems to be that CAR is presumptively reasonable—a presumption that the human eye and brain (perhaps undeservedly) currently enjoy. The judiciary has proven aware, at least conceptually, of CAR and its potential application in litigation. The defensibility of the concept of CAR is morphing into a footnote point. Although this does not mean CAR cannot be challenged (or that it should not be challenged in action), challenges only to the general concept of CAR now tend to die quickly on the vine when raised.

11.7 CONCLUSION

Big Data leaves room for big electronic discovery mistakes. In preservation, make sure to flip the "off" switch for automatic deletion protocols when appropriate; to properly implement, track, and lift litigation holds; and to ensure that collection is handled in a forensically sound and defensible manner. Loop in the lawyers in implementing Big Data analytics to ensure you have considered the legal ramifications (and propriety) of the analytics, as well as automating, where possible, data preservation. Resist overly broad Big Database discovery and be specific in seeking to obtain or block discovery requests. When drowning in Big Data search, use CAR in the right cases to do a better job for a lower cost—and make sure to have a clawback in place in federal litigations involving high-volume exchanges of electronically stored information.

NOTES

1. IBM. Apply New Analytics Tools to Reveal New Opportunities. n.d. http://www.ibm.com/smarterplanet/us/en/business_analytics/article/it_business_intelligence.html.
2. *Armory* is a story about a chimney sweep's boy and jeweler. Armory was a chimney sweep's boy who happened on a ring containing a jewel. Not knowing the jewel's value, Armory took the ring to a jeweler, Delamirie. Delamirie's assistant removed the gem from the ring, telling Armory he wished to weigh the jewel to determine its worth. The assistant brought back the ring—with the jewel missing from the socket—and told Armory the ring was only worth three half-pence. Armory asked for the ring and jewel back; Delamirie's assistant apparently "lost" the ring. Delamirie (and his assistant, as his agent) had a duty to preserve the jewel, and as they failed to produce the jewel for inspection, the chief justice instructed the jury that "unless the defendant did produce the jewel, and shew it not to be of the finest water, they should presume the strongest case against him, and make the value of the best jewels the measure of their damages: which they accordingly did." This sanction is known as an "adverse inference[,]" and spoliation is not a new concept at law.
3. See *Pillay v. Millard Refrigerated Services, Inc.*, 2013 U.S. Dist. LEXIS 72350 (N.D. Ill 2013).
4. *Cache La Poudre Feeds, LLC v. Land O'Lakes Farmland Feed, LLC*, 244 F.R.D. 614, 629 (D. Colo. 2007), citing *In re Cheyenne Software, Inc.*, 1997 U.S. Dist. LEXIS 2414 (E.D. N.Y. 1997) (awarding monetary sanctions based on defendants' destruction

of documents stored on computer hard drives; noted that information on those hard drives could have been copied to other relatively inexpensive storage media).

5. *Samsung Electronics Co., Ltd. v. Rambus, Inc.*, 439 F.Supp.2d 524, 565 (E.D. Va. 2006). See also *Zubulake v. UBS Warburg LLC*, 2004 WL 1620866 at *8 (S.D. N.Y. 2004) ("It is not sufficient to notify all employees of a legal hold and expect that the party will then retain and produce all relevant information. Counsel must take affirmative steps to monitor compliance so that all sources of discoverable information are identified and searched.").

6. See *Bayoil, S.A. v. Polembros Shipping Ltd.*, 196 F.R.D. 479, 483 (S.D. Tex. 2000) ("Notice does not have to be of actual litigation, but can concern 'potential' litigation. . . . Otherwise, any person could shred documents to their heart's content before suit is brought without fear of sanction.").

7. See *EEOC v. Dillon Cos., Inc.*, 839 F. Supp. 2d 1141, 1143 (D. Colo. 2011).

8. See *Ashton v. Knight Transp., Inc.*, 772 F. Supp. 2d 772, 775 (N.D. Tex. 2011).

9. See *Kraft Reinsurance Ir., Ltd., v. Pallets Acquisitions LLC*, 843 F. Supp. 2d 1318, 1320 (N.D. Ga. 2011).

10. *Combined Ins. Co. of America v. Wiest*, 578 F. Supp. 2d 822, 826 (W.D. Va. 2008).

11. See *Hynix Semiconductor Inc. v. Rambus, Inc.*, 591 F. Supp. 1038, 1061 (N.D. Cal. 2006) (noting "Litigation 'is an everpresent possibility in American life" and that reasonable anticipation requires "more than a possibility" of litigation).

12. Carter Jernigan and Behram F.T. Mistree. Gaydar: Facebook Friendships Expose Sexual Orientation. *First Monday*, 14(10) (October 5, 2009). http://firstmonday.org/article/view/2611/2302.

13. *In re Ford Motor Co.*, 345 F. 3d 1315, 1316-17 (11th Cir. 2003).

14. *Advanced Tactical Ordnance Sys., LLC v. Real Action Paintball, Inc.*, 2013 U.S. Dist. LEXIS 25022 (N.D. Ind. 2013).

15. See, for example, *Mills v. Billington*, 2013 U.S. Dist. LEXIS 118284 (D.D.C. 2013) (noting in addressing database discovery issues that "electronic discovery issues in this case have been unnecessarily complicated, the Plaintiffs identified what they sought but failed to do so with precision, and the Defendant expressed an inability to understand Plaintiffs' request and failed to inform the Court or the Plaintiffs when the data was no longer preserved in its possession.").

16. See *In Re Fannie Mae Securities Litigation*, 2009 U.S. App. LEXIS 9 (D.C. Cir. 2009).

17. *S2 Automation LLC v. Micron Technology, Inc.*, 2012 U.S. Dist. LEXIS 120097 (D.N.M. 2012).

18. *Robocast, Inc. v. Apple, Inc.*, No. 11-235 (D. Del.) December 5, 2012, transcript at 16:4–8.

Glossary

aggregated data: Refers to data that has been scrubbed of any personally or entity identifiable information and then generally combined with similar information from other parties.

anonymization: The process of deidentifying personally identifiable information such that no code or other association for reidentification exists.

audit trail: An automatic feature of computer operating systems or certain programs that creates a record of transactions relating to a file, piece of data, or particular user.

authentication: Verification of the identity of a user, process, or device, often as a prerequisite to allowing access to resources in an information system.

backups: Duplicate copies of data, generally stored at an off-site, secure facility.

Big Data: A process to deliver decision-making insights. The process uses people and technology to quickly analyze large amounts of data of different types (traditional table structured data and unstructured data, such as pictures, video, email, and Tweets) from a variety of sources to produce a stream of actionable knowledge.

bit: The smallest unit of data. A bit can have only one of two values: 1 or 0. *See* **byte**.

byte: A basic unit of data. A byte consists of eight bits and can represent a single character such as a letter or number. A *megabyte* refers to a million bytes of information. A *gigabyte* refers to a billion bytes of information.

cache: Memory used to store frequently used data. With regard to the Internet, caching refers to the process of storing popular or frequently visited websites on a hard disk or in RAM so that the next time the site is accessed it is retrieved from memory rather than from the Internet. Caching is used to reduce traffic on the Internet and to vastly decrease the time it takes to access a Web site.

central processing unit: Abbreviated CPU. The portion of a computer that controls the processing and storage of data.

certificate: A digital representation of information that at least (1) identifies the certification authority issuing it, (2) names or identifies its subscriber, (3) contains the subscriber's public key, (4) identifies its operational period, and (5) is digitally signed by the certification authority.

click-wrap agreement: An agreement that is presented to the user for acceptance by clicking on "I Accept" or similar means. The agreement is usually presented to the user as part of the installation process for a piece of software or as part of the registration process when a user is accessing an online service.

client computer: A personal computer or workstation connected to a network file server. *See* **file server.**

client-server network: A type of network in which server computers provide files to client computers. *See* **client computer** and **file server**.

cloud computing: A delivery model for information technology resources and services that uses the Internet to provide immediately scalable and rapidly provisioned resources as services using a subscription or utility-based fee structure.

compliance: Conformity in fulfilling official requirements.

compressed file: A file whose contents have been "compressed" using specialized software so that it occupies less storage space than in its uncompressed state. Files are typically compressed to save disk storage space or to decrease the amount of time required to send them over a communications network like the Internet.

consequential damages: Are damages that are not a direct result of an act but a consequence of that act. Consequential damages must be foreseeable at the time the contract is entered into. In connection with a breach of contract, consequential damages would include any loss the breaching party had reason to know of and that could not reasonably be prevented by the nonbreaching party. Consequential damages can include loss of business, loss of profits, and harm to business reputation.

cookie: A cookie is a small data file that a website can store on a visitor's computer. If the visitor returns to the website, the cookie can be used to identify the visitor and to provide personalized information to the visitor. Cookies are used by the operators of websites as marketing tools to gain information about their visitors and to track their movements on the site. Web browsers can be configured to reject cookies when they are offered.

CPU: Acronym for central processing unit. *See* **central processing unit**.

data flow map: Data flow maps are tools that graphically represent the results of a comprehensive data assessment to illustrate what information comes into an organization, for what purposes that information is used, and who has access to that information. Use of a data map can help ensure that an organization is in compliance with applicable law, the organization's privacy and information security policies, and contractual obligations.

data mining or text mining: The analysis of raw data to produce results specific to a particular inquiry (e.g., how often a particular word is used, whether a particular product is in demand, how a particular consumer reacts to advertisements).

deidentification: The process of removing or obscuring personally identifiable information such that the information does not identify an individual and there is no reasonable basis to believe that the information can be used to identify an individual.

direct damages: Direct damages are intended to place the nonbreaching party in the position it would have occupied had the breaching party performed as promised under their contract. They are generally the difference between the value of the performance received and the value of the performance promised as measured by contract or market value. They are not intended to punish the breaching party.

disk mirroring: A method of protecting data from a catastrophic hard disk failure. As each file is stored on the hard disk, an identical, "mirror," copy is made on a second hard disk or on a different partition of the same disk. If the first disk fails, the data can be recovered instantly from the mirror disk. Mirroring is a standard feature in most network operating systems.

encryption: A method of using mathematical algorithms to encode a message or data file so that it cannot be understood without a password.

exabyte: A unit of measure for computer storage. 1 exabyte (EB) = 1,000,000,000,000,000,000 bytes = 10^{18} bytes = 1,000 petabytes = 1 billion gigabytes.

extranet: An extension of the corporate intranet over the Internet so that vendors, business partners, customers, and others can have access to the intranet. *See* **intranet** and **Internet**.

field(s): Individual entries or groups of entries within a file relating to the same subject. For example, a litigation support database may have fields for the creator and recipient of a document and its subject.

file: A collection of data or information stored under a specified name on a disk. Examples of files are programs, data files, spreadsheets, databases, and word-processing documents.

file server: A central computer used to store files (e.g., data, word-processing documents, programs) for use by client computers connected to a network. Most file servers run special operating systems known as network operating systems (NOS). Novell Netware and Windows NT are common NOS. *See* **client computer** and **client-server network**.

hard disk: A storage device based on a fixed, permanently mounted disk drive. Hard disks can be either internal or external to the computer.

IaaS: The capability provided to the customer regarding provision processing, storage, networks, and other fundamental computing resources where the consumer is able to deploy and run arbitrary software, which can include operating systems and applications. The consumer does not manage or control the underlying cloud infrastructure but has control over operating systems, storage, and deployed applications and possibly limited control of select networking components (e.g., host firewalls).

International Organization for Standardization (ISO): An international organization created for the purpose of developing various families of voluntary standards for information security, disaster recovery, business continuity, quality management, risk management, and others.

Internet: A global collection of interconnected computers and networks that use the TCP/IP (Transmission Control Protocol/Internet Protocol) to communicate with each other. At one time, the term *Internet* was used as an acronym for "interconnected networks."

Internet of Things: The Internet of Things refers to a computing concept by which uniquely identifiable objects are able to identify themselves to and communicate with other devices over the Internet.

intranet: A computer network designed to be used within a business or company. An intranet is so named because it uses much of the same technology as the Internet. Web browsers, email, newsgroups, HTML documents, and websites are all found on intranets.

In addition, the method for transmitting information on these networks is TCP/IP (Transmission Control Protocol/Internet Protocol). *See* **Internet**.

LAN: Acronym for local-area network. *See* **local-area network**.

license agreement: A contract that defines the scope of activities a licensee can engage in with regard to the database (e.g., use the data solely for internal use, distribute limited segments to others, combine the database with other data, etc.).

licensee: The party in a license agreement that is granted the right to use a database.

licensor: The party in a license agreement that owns the database and is granting a third party the right to use it.

local-area network: Abbreviated LAN. A network of computers and other devices generally located within a relatively limited area (e.g., within a particular office, building, or group of buildings).

log file: A record of activity or transactions that occur on a particular computer system.

metadata: Data about data. For example, it can refer to application metadata, which is embedded in the file it describes (such as information about the person who created the document, the date and time of creation, the number of times the document was edited and by whom, and the program used to create the document), or system metadata, which includes information about computer files not embedded within the file itself (such as information in a computer's master file management system containing data regarding a file's location, name, date of creation, modification, and access).

network map: A network map is a graphical depiction of the way in which the various computers, file servers, and peripherals on a network are interconnected. The map typically identifies the type and speed (bandwidth) of the connections.

NDA: An acronym for nondisclosure agreement. *See* **nondisclosure agreement**.

nondisclosure agreement (NDA): An agreement, generally entered into at an early stage in a potential engagement, that governs the parties' respective confidentiality obligations.

NOS: Acronym for network operating system. *See* **file server**.

object code: The machine-readable version of a computer program. *See* **source code**.

offshore: In the context of a professional service engagement, contractors who are located outside the United States.

Open Source: A program in which the source code is available to the general public for use or modification from its original design free of charge. Common Open Source licenses include the GNU General Public License, GNU Library General Public License, Artistic License, BSD license, Mozilla Public License, and other similar licenses listed at http://www.opensource.org/licenses. Open Source code is typically created as a collaborative effort in which programmers improve on the code and share the changes within the community.

operating system: Abbreviated OS. A program used to control the basic operation of a computer (e.g., storing and retrieving data from memory, controlling how information is displayed on the computer monitor, operating the central processing unit, and communicating with peripherals).

PaaS: The capability provided to the customer to deploy onto the cloud infrastructure customer-created or acquired applications created using programming languages and tools supported by the provider. The consumer does not manage or control the underlying cloud infrastructure, including network, servers, operating systems, or storage, but has control over the deployed applications and possibly application hosting environment configurations.

PC: Acronym for personal computer.

partition: A region of a hard disk treated by the computer's operating system as a separate drive. Through the use of partitions, a computer with a single hard disk can appear to have two or more drives.

Payment Card Industry Data Security Standards (PCI DSS): A robust and comprehensive set of standards and supporting materials created by the PCI Security Standards Council to enhance payment card data security.

peer-to-peer network: A type of network in which a group of personal computers is interconnected so that the hard disks, CD ROMs, files, and printers of each computer can be accessed from every other computer on the network. Peer-to-peer networks do not have a central file server. This type of system is used if less than a dozen computers will be networked.

personal digital assistant: Abbreviated PDA. PDAs range from compact personal electronic organizers (e.g., calendars, phone lists, brief notes) to the new breed of palm-size computers that are capable of running full-featured word-processing programs and spreadsheets and of browsing the Internet and sending and receiving email. These devices can hold hundreds, and soon thousands, of pages of information.

petabyte: A unit of measure for computer storage. 1 petabyte (PB) = 1,000,000,000,000,000 bytes = 10^{15} bytes = 1,000 terabytes.

proxy server: A server used to manage Internet-related traffic coming to and from a local-area network; can provide certain functionality (e.g., access control and caching of popular websites).

public key cryptography: An encryption method that uses a two-part key: a public key and a private key. Users generally distribute their public key but keep their private key to themselves. This is also known as **asymmetric cryptography**.

RAM: Acronym for random access memory. *See* **random access memory**.

random access memory: Abbreviated RAM. An integrated circuit into which data can be read or written by a microprocessor or other device. The memory is volatile and will be lost if the system is disconnected from its power source.

read-only memory: Abbreviated ROM. An integrated circuit into which information, data, or programs are permanently stored. The absence of electric current will not result in loss of memory.

ROM: Acronym for read-only memory. *See* **read-only memory**.

SaaS: Abbreviation for software as a service. It is the capability provided to the consumer to use the provider's applications running on a cloud infrastructure. The applications are accessible from various client devices through a thin client interface such as a web browser (e.g., web-based email). The consumer does not manage or control the underlying cloud infrastructure, including network, servers, operating systems, storage, or even individual application capabilities, with the possible exception of limited user-specific application configuration settings.

shrink-wrap agreement: An agreement that is included as part of the packaging or in the documentation accompanying a piece of software or equipment. In some cases, the CD containing the software may be provided in an envelope with the shrink-wrap agreement printed on the outside. Opening of the envelope indicates the user's acceptance of the terms.

source code: The version of a computer program that can be read by humans. The source code is translated into machine-readable code by a program called a *compiler*. Access to the source code is required to understand how a computer program works or to modify the program. *See* **object code**.

stand-alone computer: A personal computer that is not connected to any other computer or network, except possibly through a modem.

structure databases: Databases with a high degree of organization, with designated data fields and defined relationships between the data fields.

sublicense: The ability of a party who is, itself, a licensee of a database to, in turn, grant licenses to the database to third parties.

terabyte: A unit of measure for computer storage. 1 terabyte (TB) = 1,000,000,000,000 bytes = 10^{12} bytes = 1,000 gigabytes.

third party: An entity that is not in contractual privity (e.g., a typical vendor subcontractor is not a party to the agreement between the vendor and the customer). In these situations, it is not possible to directly enforce the contract against the third party.

trending: A colloquialism to describe the popularity of an item (usually in social media) (e.g., if a topic is popular, it is "trending").

unstructured databases: Are the opposite of structured databases. The data is raw and unorganized, making it difficult to search by traditional methods.

WAN: Acronym for wide-area network. *See* **wide-area network**.

web browser: A program used to view HTML pages on the World Wide Web.

web server: A computer on which a website is stored.

website: A collection of related HTML documents stored on the same computer and accessible to users of the Internet.

web-wrap agreement: A click-wrap agreement or other form of terms and conditions presented to the user in connection with use of a website or online service. The standard terms and conditions of use commonly found as a hyperlink on the first page of a website are an example of a web-wrap agreement.

wide-area network: Abbreviated WAN. A network of computers and other devices distributed over a broad geographic area.

workstation: A personal computer connected to a network. A workstation can also refer to a high-performance computer used for intensive graphics or numerical calculations.

yottabyte: A unit of measure for computer storage. 1 yottabyte (YB) = 1,000,000,000,000,000,000,000,000 bytes = 10^{24} bytes = 1,000 zettabytes.

zettabyte: A unit of measure for computer storage. 1 zettabyte (ZB) = 1,000,000,000,000,000,000,000 bytes = 10^{21} bytes = 1,000 exabytes = 1 billion terabytes.

Index